Hebrews

The True Messiah

Group Directory

Pass this Directory around and have your Group Members
fill in their names and phone numbers

Name   **Phone**

_____   _____

_____   _____

_____   _____

_____   _____

_____   _____

_____   _____

_____   _____

_____   _____

_____   _____

_____   _____

_____   _____

_____   _____

_____   _____

Hebrews

EDITING AND PRODUCTION TEAM:
James F. Couch, Jr., Sharon Penington, Cathy Tardif,
Erika Tiepel, Katharine Harris, Ben Colter, Scott Lee

Hebrews - The True Messiah
© 2003, 1998, 1988 Serendipity House
Reprinted March 2005

Published by Serendipity House Publishers
Nashville, Tennessee

ISBN: 1-5749-4094-5

To purchase additional copies of this resource or other studies:
ORDER ONLINE at www.SerendipityHouse.com
WRITE Serendipity House, 117 10th Avenue North, Nashville, TN 37234
FAX (615) 277-8181
PHONE (800) 525-9563

1-800-525-9563
www.SerendipityHouse.com

Printed in the United States of America
11 10 09 08 07 06   4 5 6 7 8 9 10 11

Table of Contents

Core Values

Community: The purpose of this curriculum is to build community within the body of believers around Jesus Christ.

Group Process: To build community, the curriculum must be designed to take a group through a step-by-step process of sharing your story with one another.

Interactive Bible Study: To share your "story," the approach to Scripture in the curriculum needs to be open-ended and right brain—to "level the playing field" and encourage everyone to share.

Developmental Stages: To provide a healthy program throughout the four stages of the life cycle of a group, the curriculum needs to offer courses on three levels of commitment: (1) Beginner Level—low-level entry, high structure, to level the playing field; (2) Growth Level—deeper Bible study, flexible structure, to encourage group accountability; (3) Discipleship Level—in-depth Bible study, open structure, to move the group into high gear.

Target Audiences: To build community throughout the culture of the church, the curriculum needs to be flexible, adaptable and transferable into the structure of the average church.

Mission: To expand the Kingdom of God one person at a time by filling the "empty chair." (We add an extra chair to each group session to remind us of our mission.)

Introduction

Each healthy small group will move through various stages as it matures.

Multiply Stage: The group begins the multiplication process. Members pray about their involvement in new groups. The "new" groups begin the life cycle again with the Birth Stage.

Birth Stage: This is the time in which group members form relationships and begin to develop community. The group will spend more time in ice-breaker exercises, relational Bible study and covenant building.

Develop Stage: The inductive Bible study deepens while the group members discover and develop gifts and skills. The group explores ways to invite their neighbors and coworkers to group meetings.

Growth Stage: Here the group begins to care for one another as it learns to apply what they learn through Bible study, worship and prayer.

Subgrouping: If you have nine or more people at a meeting, Serendipity recommends you divide into subgroups of 3–6 for the Bible study. Ask one person to be the leader of each subgroup and to follow the directions for the Bible study. After 30 minutes, the Group Leader will call "time" and ask all subgroups to come together for the Caring Time.

Each group meeting should include all parts of the "three-part agenda."

 Ice-Breaker: Fun, history-giving questions are designed to warm the group and to build understanding about the other group members. You can choose to use all of the Ice-Breaker questions, especially if there is a new group member that will need help in feeling comfortable with the group.

 Bible Study: The heart of each meeting is the reading and examination of the Bible. The questions are open, discover questions that lead to further inquiry. Reference notes are provided to give everyone a "level playing field." The emphasis is on understanding what the Bible says and applying the truth to real life. The questions for each session build. There is always at least one "going deeper" question provided. You should always leave time for the last of the "questions for interaction." Should you choose, you can use the optional "going deeper" question to satisfy the desire for the challenging questions in groups that have been together for a while.

 Caring Time: All study should point us to actions. Each session ends with prayer and direction in caring for the needs of the group members. You can choose between several questions. You should always pray for the "empty chair." Who do you know that could fill that void in your group?

Sharing Your Story: These sessions are designed for members to share a little of their personal lives each time. Through a number of special techniques, each member is encouraged to move from low risk, less personal sharing to higher risk responses. This helps develop the sense of community and facilitates caregiving.

Group Covenant: A group covenant is a "contract" that spells out your expectations and the ground rules for your group. It's very important that your group discuss these issues—preferably as part of the first session.

Ground Rules:

• Priority: While you are in the group, you give the group meeting priority.

• Participation: Everyone participates and no one dominates.

• Respect: Everyone is given the right to their own opinion and all questions are encouraged and respected.

• Confidentiality: Anything that is said in the meeting is never repeated outside the meeting.

• Empty Chair: The group stays open to new people at every meeting.

• Support: Permission is given to call upon each other in time of need—even in the middle of the night.

• Advice Giving: Unsolicited advice is not allowed.

• Mission: We agree to do everything in our power to start a new group as our mission.

Issues:

• The time and place this group is going to meet is _____.

• Refreshments are _____ responsibility.

• Child care is _____ responsibility.

SESSION 1
THE SUPERIORITY OF THE SON
SCRIPTURE HEBREWS 1:1–14

Welcome to this study of Hebrews. Together we will study this marvelous portrait of Jesus Christ as seen through the lens of the Old Testament. We will be encouraged and reassured that Jesus is truly the way, the truth and the life. In the first chapter, the author of Hebrews emphasizes that Jesus is superior to the prophets and angels, through whom God's Word had previously been conveyed.

No one knows who wrote the epistle to the Hebrews. The author is nowhere named within it, nor is there any strong external evidence pointing to one particular person. These facts have not deterred speculation, however, and at least seven possibilities have been proposed—Paul, Barnabas (Acts 4:36), Luke, Priscilla, Silas (1 Peter 5:12), Apollos (Acts 18:24), and Clement of Rome.

As with so much else about this epistle, it is difficult to be certain about its date of composition. If the persecution referred to is that of Nero, then Hebrews was written after A.D. 64. Some hold that it must have been written prior to the fall of Jerusalem and the destruction of the temple in A.D. 70, for such an unprecedented event would probably have been mentioned by the book's author as the sure sign of the end of the sacrificial system.

The theme of the book is the superiority of Jesus to all that has gone before. He is superior to the prophets (1:1–3), the angels (1:4–2:18), Moses (3:1–19), and the high priests of the old covenant (4:14–8:13).

The purpose of the book is to keep Christians true in a time of persecution. The author wisely begins by pointing the readers to Jesus, the only one who is worth the high cost of allegiance that they might have to pay. As a result, in the book of Hebrews we get a beautiful picture of Christ—the prophet, priest and king whose new covenant is so superior to the old covenant that to fall away from him should be unthinkable.

The title "To the Hebrews" can be traced back to manuscripts of the late second century. Even though it was not part of the original document, it seems to be accurate, given the very Jewish flavor of the epistle. This letter was probably written to a particular assembly of Jewish-Christian believers (perhaps a house church) that was part of a larger community, quite possibly in Rome.

Whoever these people were, it is clear that they had suffered great persecution (10:32–34), and that they were being tempted to abandon Christianity. The temptation to give up their faith was severe enough that the letter to the Hebrews had to be written to encourage these beleaguered believers to "hold on" (3:6), to "persevere" (10:36), and to "hold unswervingly to the hope we profess" (10:23), lest they compromise Christ and lose all the enormous blessings of the new covenant.

The book of Hebrews is full of strange allusions that are foreign to our understanding and culture. However, if we take the time to look carefully at those allusions, we can find some eternal understandings that have meaning for us today.

Although Hebrews has been called an epistle, it lacks several key features of a true letter. It has no ordinary greeting, nor does it name either the sender or the recipients. There are no personal references in the letter until the end, where we find personal greetings and a standard conclusion.

If Hebrews is not a true letter, then what is it? Some have suggested that Hebrews is a written sermon. Its method of argument is sermonic in nature. Structurally, its closest New Testament parallel is 1 John, which also seems to be a sermon.

ICE-BREAKER   15 Min.
CONNECT WITH YOUR GROUP

. . . .

LEADER

Be sure to read the introductory pages in the front of this book prior to this first session. To help your group members get acquainted, have each person introduce him or herself and then take turns answering one or two of the Ice-Breaker questions. If time allows, you may want to discuss all three questions.

Hebrews compares Jesus to many other persons through whom God's message has come. With whom have you been compared? Take some time to get to know one another better by sharing your responses to the following questions.

1. To whom did you get compared when you were a child?
❏ An older sibling.
❏ A parent.
❏ Another child in the neighborhood.
❏ Other _____.

2. When you were a teenager and your parents wanted to make sure a message got through to you, how did they most often convey it?
❏ By yelling.
❏ By a note on the refrigerator door.
❏ By a long, drawn-out lecture.
❏ Other _____.

3. When you were a child or teen did you ever receive accolades for any musical, dramatic, athletic or academic performance? Did your parent(s) save any mementos of this time?

BIBLE STUDY

READ SCRIPTURE AND DISCUSS

30 Min.

LEADER

Ask two members of the group, selected ahead of time, to read aloud the Scripture passage. Have one read the part of the author, and the other read the quotes in verses 5–13. Then discuss the questions that follow, dividing into subgroups of four or five as necessary. Be sure to save at least 15 minutes for the Caring Time.

Hebrews begins with a beautiful description of Jesus Christ, pointing to him as the way to God and the ultimate fulfillment of all prophecy. He is particularly superior to the angels as he is God's Son and sits at "the right hand of the Majesty in heaven" (v. 3). Read Hebrews 1:1–14 and note the many ways that God reveals himself to us.

The Son Superior to Angels

Prophets – "to speak for"
Angels – "messengers"

Reader 1:   **1** *In the past God spoke to our forefathers through the prophets at many times and in various ways, ²but in these last days he has spoken to us by his Son, whom he appointed heir of all things, and through whom he made the universe. ³ The Son is the radiance of God's glory and the* <u>exact representation</u> *of his being,* <u>sustaining</u> *all things by his powerful word. After he had provided purification for sins, he sat down at the right hand of the Majesty in heaven. ⁴So he became as much superior to the angels as the* <u>name</u> *he has inherited is superior to theirs. ⁵For to which of the angels did God ever say,*

(Creating+)

Reader 2:   *"You are my Son; today I have become your Father"?*

Reader 1:   *Or again,*

Reader 2:   *"I will be his Father, and he will be my Son"?*   v. 5   ① *God's son.*

Reader 1:   *⁶And again, when God brings his firstborn into the world, he says,*

Reader 2:   *"Let all God's angels worship him."*   v. 6   ② *Higher than angels.*

Reader 1:   *⁷In speaking of the angels he says,*

Reader 2:   *"He makes his angels winds, his servants flames of fire."*

Reader 1:   *⁸But about the Son he says,*

Reader 2:   *"Your throne, O God, will last for ever and ever,*
and righteousness will be the scepter of your kingdom.
⁹You have loved righteousness and hated wickedness;

③ Elevated above *v.9*
all.

therefore God, your God, has set you above your companions
by anointing you with the oil of joy."

Reader 1:   ¹⁰He also says,

Reader 2:   "In the beginning, O Lord, you laid the foundations of the earth,
④ Eternal.   and the heavens are the work of your hands.
v. 10-12   ¹¹They will perish, but you remain; they will all wear out like a garment.
            ¹²You will roll them up like a robe; like a garment they will be changed.
            But you remain the same, and your years will never end."

Reader 1:   ¹³To which of the angels did God ever say,

v.13
Reader 2:   "Sit at my right hand until I make your enemies
⑤ Highest honor   a footstool for your feet"?
given by God.
Reader 1:   ¹⁴Are not all angels ministering spirits sent to serve those who will inher-
            it salvation?

Hebrews 1:1–14

LEADER

Refer to the Summary and Study Notes at the end of this session as needed. If 30 minutes is not enough time to answer all of the questions in this section, conclude the Bible Study by answering question #7.

QUESTIONS FOR INTERACTION

1. How has God spoken to his people in the past? How does this compare to the unique way he has spoken through Jesus?

2. What past achievement and future honor does the author credit to the Son (v. 2)? What does John say in John 1:3 of the achievement to which this passage refers?

3. What "seat of honor" has Christ been given (vv. 3,13)? What is the significance of that position (see notes on v. 3)?

4. What was the Son's final achievement before sitting down at the right hand of God? How did he accomplish this achievement?

5. What are three or four accolades that are given in this Scripture to God's Son that are not given to angels?

6. How has God spoken to you in the past and which way comes across most clearly?
   ❏ Through Scripture.
   ❏ Through a person.

❏ Through a dream.

❏ Other _____.

7. If you could have angels or "ministering spirits" come to you right now, what need would you want them to minister to?

GOING DEEPER: *If your group has time and/or wants a challenge, go on to this question.*

8. What does it mean that the Son is the "radiance of God's glory and the exact representation of his being" (v. 3)? How is this like/different from what is said of humankind in general in Genesis 1:27?

CARING TIME   15 Min.

APPLY THE LESSON AND PRAY FOR ONE ANOTHER

LEADER

Take some extra time in this first session to go over the introductory material at the beginning of this book. At the close, pass around your books and have everyone sign the Group Directory at the beginning of this book.

This very important time is for developing and expressing your concern for each other as group members by praying for one another.

1. Agree on the group covenant and ground rules (see the front of this book).

2. Begin the prayer time by taking turns and completing the following sentence: "I would like God to speak to me and give me guidance about ..."

3. Share any other prayer requests and praises, and then close in prayer. Pray specifically for God to lead you to someone to bring next week to fill the empty chair.

- who do you say that Jesus is?
- Why is it important to understand Jesus' superiority?
- Why is there an entire chapter explaining Jesus' superiority to angels? Specifically, how is he superior (5 ways)?

Today we were reminded that Jesus is truly God's Son and that God has spoken through him and provided a way for the purification of our sins. In the coming week, be sure to take some time each day not only to pray, but also to listen and be open to God's guidance. Next week we will look at the importance of the Son's message and how he is the perfect Savior for us. We will be encouraged to hold on to our precious faith and not get distracted by the world around us.

NOTES ON HEBREWS 1:1–14

Summary: One of the first things we notice about the "letter" to the Hebrews is that it doesn't start out like a letter at all. There isn't the usual address and greetings that we would expect to find in a letter. In fact, it sounds more like an essay or treatise. (Only at the end will it sound like a letter.) In any case, a modern person might find it sounding very much like an extended commercial, with the general theme of "Jesus is better than 'Brand X.'" During the course of the letter, the author will promote Jesus' superiority to the most central icons of Hebrew faith: prophets, angels, Moses and the priesthood. After implying Jesus' superiority to the prophets, most of this chapter is devoted to his superiority to angels.

It is important to the author to establish Jesus' superiority to angels because angels were believed to be the ones who conveyed the Law to the people of Israel. If indeed the Son is superior to angels, then the covenant that the Son brought and secured is a better covenant than the covenant brought through angels.

The author established through Scripture that Jesus is superior to the angels in the following ways: (1) he is designated as God's Son (v. 5); (2) he is referred to as one to be worshiped by angels (v. 6); (3) he is to be elevated above all others (v. 9); (4) he is eternal (vv. 10–12); and (5) he is given a place of honor at the right hand of God (vv. 3,13).

1:1 *through the prophets.* The prophets were honored as those whom the Lord sent to speak to his people in times of need. The word "prophet" means "speaks for," and hence a prophet is one who speaks for God.

1:2 *but.* In contrast to the partial, limited revelation of the prophets, the Son fully reveals God to the world. ***last days.*** This term signifies the time after Jesus' resurrection. Now that the Messiah had come, there was an expectation of a speedy culmination of history (Acts 2:17). ***he has spoken.*** By the description of Christ that follows, the author intends to show that the word of God communicated through Jesus is superior to all the forms of communication used in the past. ***through whom he made the universe.*** See John 1:1–3.

1:3 *the radiance of God's glory.* God's glory is like light that radiates from its source (Ex. 24:17; 34:29–35). Jesus' miracles revealed God's glory (John 2:11), and thus made God known to the people (John 1:18). ***exact representation.*** The Greek word *charakter* is used in engraving dies used for stamps. Whatever is stamped bears the same image as is on the die. In the same way, the Son fully bears the nature of God (Col. 1:15; 2:9). ***sustaining all things by his powerful word.*** The Son's role in creation was not limited to creation's origin or its future. It is his powerful word that keeps order and stability in creation (Col. 1:17). ***purification for sins.*** While popular thought held that people had to work for their own purification from sin, the author uses a term related to the Day of Atonement to show that the Son has dealt with sin. The Day of Atonement provides the major interpretive grid for this author's understanding of the meaning of Jesus' death (see chapters 7–10). ***the right hand.*** This is the position of honor and power beside a king, and a position reserved for the king's most trusted advisor. It accents the Son's royal dominion.

1:4 The Son, superior to the prophets (v. 1), is also superior to the angels. ***the name he has inherited.*** The name of "Son" is greater than that of "messenger," which is what "angel" means. See also Philippians 2:4–11, especially verse 9.

1:8–9 This quote (Ps. 45:6–7) directly attributes deity to the Son.

1:14 In contrast to the ruling authority of the Son, the function of the angels is to serve his people at the Son's command. ***ministering.*** This word describes the priestly service at the tabernacle (8:4–6). In the New Testament, angels perform tasks such as interceding for children (Matt. 18:10), protecting the apostles (Acts 12:7–10), revealing God's will (Luke 1:11–38; Acts 8:26), and carrying out God's judgment (Rev. 7:1). ***salvation.*** Later passages indicate the author viewed salvation as a deliverance (from the devil's power—2:14; the fear of death—2:15; and the power of sin—9:26) leading to holiness (10:10), forgiveness (10:18), free access to God (10:22), and the eternal inheritance, which God provides for those who have faith (9:15).

SESSION 2
A PERFECT SAVIOR

SCRIPTURE   HEBREWS 2:1–18

LAST WEEK

In last week's session we heard a beautiful description of Jesus and considered what it means that he is the "radiance of God's glory" (1:3), superior to the prophets and angels. This week we will explore what this implies about the Son's message and his role as our Savior. We will learn to particularly appreciate how he took on death itself for our benefit.

ICE-BREAKER   15 Min.
CONNECT WITH YOUR GROUP

LEADER

Begin the session with a word of prayer. Have your group members take turns sharing their responses to one, two or all three of the Ice-Breaker questions. Be sure that everyone gets a chance to participate.

In the passage for this week we will be exploring how the Son helps us deal with temptation and death because of his authority over those two oppressors. What has been your experience with authority, temptation and death? Get to know each other better by sharing some of your unique life experiences.

1. Who is presently subject to you—under your authority?

2. What was the first experience you remember having with death as a child?

3. What kind of temptation did you wrestle with most frequently as a child?
   ❐ The temptation to lie.
   ❐ The temptation to take things that didn't belong to you.
   ❐ The temptation to get into fights.
   ❐ Other _____.

BIBLE STUDY

READ SCRIPTURE AND DISCUSS

30 Min.

LEADER

Select two members of the group ahead of time to read aloud the Scripture passage. Have one person read verses 1–9, and the other read verses 10–18. Then divide into subgroups of four or five and discuss the Questions for Interaction.

The implication of the truth that the Son is superior to the angels and prophets is now revealed: we must pay very careful attention to his message and what God did through him. God made Jesus <u>a perfect Savior for us</u> by having him experience everything we experience—including temptation, suffering and death. Only in this way could he be victorious and make atonement for the sins of the people. Read Hebrews 2:1–18 and note how Jesus is not only our Savior, but also our brother.

Jesus Made Like His Brothers

2 We must pay more careful attention, therefore, to what we have heard, so that we do not drift away. ²For if the message spoken by angels was binding, and every violation and disobedience received its just punishment, ³how shall we escape if we ignore such a great salvation? This salvation, which was first announced by the Lord, was confirmed to us by those who heard him. ⁴God also testified to it by signs, wonders and various miracles, and gifts of the Holy Spirit distributed according to his will.

⁵It is not to angels that he has subjected the world to come, about which we are speaking.

⁶But there is a place where someone has testified:

"What is man that you are mindful of him,
the son of man that you care for him?
⁷You made him a little lower than the angels;
you crowned him with glory and honor
⁸ and put everything under his feet."

In putting everything under him, God left nothing that is not subject to him. Yet at present we do not see everything subject to him. ⁹But we see Jesus, who was made a little lower than the angels, now crowned with glory and honor because he suffered death, so that by the grace of God he might taste death for everyone.

¹⁰In bringing many sons to glory, it was fitting that God, for whom and through whom everything exists, should make the author of their salvation perfect through suffering. ¹¹Both the one who makes men holy and those who are made holy are of the same family. So Jesus is not ashamed to call them brothers. ¹²He says,

"I will declare your name to my brothers;
in the presence of the congregation I will sing your praises."

[13]And again,

"I will put my trust in him."

And again he says,

"Here am I, and the children God has given me."
[14]Since the children have flesh and blood, he too shared in their humanity so that by his death he might destroy him who holds the power of death—that is, the devil—[15]and free those who all their lives were held in slavery by their fear of death. [16]For surely it is not angels he helps, but Abraham's descendants. [17]For this reason he had to be made like his brothers in every way, in order that he might become a merciful and faithful high priest in service to God, and that he might make atonement for the sins of the people. [18]Because he himself suffered when he was tempted, he is able to help those who are being tempted.

Hebrews 2:1–18

QUESTIONS FOR INTERACTION

LEADER

Refer to the Summary and Study Notes at the end of this session as needed. If 30 minutes is not enough time to answer all of the questions in this section, conclude the Bible Study by answering question #7.

1. Which of the following topics dealt with in this chapter is of most concern to you right now?
   ❐ The possibility of drifting away from the faith (v. 1).
   ❐ The presence of evil in a world that is not yet subject to Christ (v. 8).
   ❐ Fear of death (vv. 9,14–15).
   ❐ How Christ helps us with temptation (vv. 17–18).

2. What helps to keep us from "drifting away"? What disciplines should a person develop to be able to "pay more careful attention"?

3. What testimony do we have that the salvation brought by Jesus Christ is true (vv. 2–4)?

4. If God's intent is to have everything subject to Jesus Christ, why is it that "at present we do not see everything subject to him" (v. 8)? How do you feel about the fact that there is so much in the world that is not yet made subject to God in Christ?

5. In what way did suffering make Christ "perfect" (see note on v. 10)? How does what the author says in verses 14–18 relate to this?

6. How does Christ "free those who all their lives were held in slavery by their fear of death" (v. 15)?

7. How free do you see yourself being right now from slavery to the fear of death, and what needs to happen for you to find greater freedom in this area of your life?

❏ Totally free—like a prisoner who has been pardoned.

❏ Well, maybe partially free, like someone on "work release" or at a "halfway house."

❏ Still in prison, but looking forward to parole soon.

❏ In prison and with a life sentence.

GOING DEEPER: *If your group has time and/or wants a challenge, go on to this question.*

8. What causes people to "drift away" from their faith? Is it possible to lose salvation by drifting away (see note on v. 1)?

CARING TIME   15 Min.
APPLY THE LESSON AND PRAY FOR ONE ANOTHER

Take some time now to encourage and support one another in a time of sharing and prayer. Remember that Jesus understands what you are going through—your trials and joys, temptations and triumphs.

1. How comfortable do you feel sharing your struggles with this group?

2. We are told, "surely it is not angels he helps, but Abraham's descendants" (v. 16). How has God helped you in the past week?

3. What can you do in the coming week to "pay more careful attention" to God and his plan for your life?

P.S. *Add new group members to the Group Directory at the front of this book.*

NEXT WEEK

Today we were cautioned that our faith is precious and, in order to prevent it from slipping away, we need to constantly pay attention to God's Word. We were also comforted by the fact that, even though the Son is superior to the angels, he is also our brother and friend. In the coming week, determine a plan of spiritual discipline that will help keep you from "drifting away." Next week we will look at how Jesus is greater than the one who had previously been the greatest deliverer in the history of the Hebrew people—Moses. We will also be warned about the consequences of unbelief and rebellion against the Son.

NOTES ON HEBREWS 2:1–18

Summary: In the first chapter we learned that the Son is superior to the angels in every way. In this chapter, the author gives the implication of that concept for his readers—the message of salvation that the Son brought is also superior to all such previous messages.

In order to be the perfect mediator of salvation, Jesus had to: (1) be commissioned by God (vv. 5–7); (2) be given authority over all things (v. 8); (3) experience all the trials and temptations that we have to experience as people, in order that he might more completely identify with us (vv. 14–18); and (4) suffer and die on our behalf, that death might be defeated. The last of these, of course, is particularly important, but it would not have been effective without the other three. Everyone suffers and dies. But since Jesus was part of God and sent by the Father to suffer and die, he is unique. He chose to do what he didn't have to do. Since he was willing to experience what we experience, he made it possible for us to identify with him, even as he identified with us. A mediator must have connection and rapport with persons on both sides of a dispute, and Jesus' suffering as a human is what made that connection.

Since Jesus is the perfect Savior, the readers should not leave their faith in him to go back to something that is in fact inferior—the old covenant. Such a relapse would most surely be punished (vv. 2–3).

2:1 so that we do not drift away. This is the first of many indications that the readers were not as steadfast as they had once been (3:14; 4:1,14; 6:11–12; 10:26–38; 12:25). The image here is one in which people neglect their spiritual condition bit by bit until they find themselves far from where they started. Does this mean a Christian can lose his or her salvation? This is a much-debated question, and a variety of verses in Hebrews are at the heart of this debate (3:12; 4:11; 6:4–20; see also John 17:11–12; 18:9).

2:2 message spoken by angels. There was a tradition of Hellenistic Judaism that angels were the ones who originally conveyed the Law on Mount Sinai.

2:3 *how shall we escape if we ignore such a great salvation?* If the means of salvation is neglected, there is no way to avoid the judgment of God. *confirmed to us by those who heard him.* This phrase indicates that the author himself was not one of the original apostles.

2:6 *there is a place where someone.* This non-specific way of referring to Scripture is typical of Hebrews (see especially 4:4). The author knew Scripture and quoted many passages, but did not even say in what book it can be found! This particular passage is from Psalm 8:4–6. While its original context was a reflection upon the significance of humanity, the author applies it to the rule of the Messiah.

2:8 *Yet at present we do not see everything subject to him.* The eventual sequence of everything being made subject to Christ can be found in 1 Corinthians 15:24–28. See also Colossians 1:15–20.

2:9 *crowned ... because he suffered death.* Jesus' death was not a denial of his glory, but the means through which his glory was revealed. *taste death for everyone.* The author hints at the purpose of Jesus' death, a theme developed more fully in chapters 7–10.

2:10 *In bringing many sons to glory.* While interpreting Psalm 8 in reference to Jesus, the author acknowledges that God's will is to exalt humanity as the crown of creation. This will be accomplished through Jesus who is the salvation brought by God. *it was fitting.* While the idea of a suffering Messiah was unknown to the Jews, the author maintains that the idea is most appropriate. *author.* Literally, "pioneer" (also 12:2). The image is of one who blazes the way, making it possible for others to follow. *make ... perfect.* This does not imply that Jesus had faults that needed to be purged. Rather, it was through suffering that Jesus was made the perfect sacrifice. Had the Son of God remained aloof from human experience and not suffered what we have to suffer, he would have not been the perfect mediator between God and us (2:14–18; 4:14–16).

2:11 *Both ... are of the same family.* This is another way of saying that Jesus shared in our humanity.

2:15 *free those who all their lives were held in slavery by their fear of death.* Jesus conquered death for all of us, so we need no longer fear its power over us (Rom. 5:16; 1 Cor. 15:20–23).

2:16 *Abraham's descendants.* Since Jewish converts were the primary audience, the author points out that it is through Jesus that the ancient promise to Abraham is fulfilled (Gen. 12:3; Rom. 2:28; 4:4–25; Gal. 3:6–14).

2:17 *like his brothers.* Because of God's choice of Israel to be his people, the Son became a flesh and blood Jew. Only in this way could he truly serve as a representative of the people before God. *a merciful and faithful high priest.* The idea of the Messiah as a high priest is this author's unique way of communicating the identity of Jesus, since it is found only here in the New Testament. *make atonement.* A priest's main function was to offer the blood of a sacrifice in place of the blood of the sinner. Chapters 9–10 interpret Jesus' death in this framework.

Session 3
A Warning Against Unbelief

Scripture Hebrews 3:1–19

LAST WEEK

In last week's session we considered how the Son was superior to the angels, and we looked at the implications of that superiority. We were also reminded that, in addition to being our Savior, Jesus is like a brother to us and understands our struggles and fears. This week we will see how he is also superior to Moses, the one who had delivered the people out of Egypt. We will also consider the seriousness of rebelling against the Son as the people rebelled against Moses in the wilderness.

ICE-BREAKER   15 Min.
Connect with Your Group

LEADER

Choose one or two Ice-Breaker questions. If you have a new group member you may want to do all three. Remember to stick closely to the three-part agenda and the time allowed for each segment.

The Bible is full of descriptions of people who rebelled against God. But then again, aren't most of us a little rebellious at some time or other? Should we get down on ourselves for having been that way, or is there a way to put it behind us? Take turns sharing how you have handled these situations in your life.

1. How would you describe the household you were part of when you were in grade school? Who was "in charge"? What did you see as your role in that household?

2. During what period of your life did you feel most rebellious, and how did you typically act out that rebellion?
    ❒ My teen years.
    ❒ College.
    ❒ Right now.
    ❒ Other _____.

3. Who is it that gives you the most encouragement when you are down on yourself? What does this person typically say or do to encourage you?

BIBLE STUDY

READ SCRIPTURE AND DISCUSS

30 Min.

LEADER

Ask two members of the group, selected ahead of time, to read aloud the Scripture passage. Have one person read the quotes from Psalm 95 in verses 7–11 and 15, and the other read the rest of the verses. Then discuss the Questions for Interaction, breaking up into smaller subgroups as necessary.

Moses was perhaps the greatest figure in the history of the Hebrew people, and the author of Hebrews was not one to put him down. He affirmed the greatness of Moses, but he went on to say that the Son is even greater. Therefore, rebelling against the Son is even more serious than the rebellion against Moses that occurred in the wilderness. Read Hebrews 3:1–19 and note the consequences of unbelief.

Warning Against Unbelief

3 *Therefore, holy brothers, who share in the heavenly calling, fix your thoughts on Jesus, the apostle and high priest whom we confess. ²He was faithful to the one who appointed him, just as Moses was faithful in all God's house. ³Jesus has been found worthy of greater honor than Moses, just as the builder of a house has greater honor than the house itself. ⁴For every house is built by someone, but God is the builder of everything. ⁵Moses was faithful as a servant in all God's house, testifying to what would be said in the future. ⁶But Christ is faithful as a son over God's house. And we are his house, if we hold on to our courage and the hope of which we boast.*

⁷So, as the Holy Spirit says:

> *"Today, if you hear his voice,*
> *⁸do not harden your hearts*
> *as you did in the rebellion,*
> *during the time of testing in the desert,*
> *⁹where your fathers tested and tried me*
> *and for forty years saw what I did.*
> *¹⁰That is why I was angry with that generation,*
> *and I said, 'Their hearts are always going astray,*
> *and they have not known my ways.'*
> *¹¹So I declared on oath in my anger,*
> *'They shall never enter my rest.' "*

¹²See to it, brothers, that none of you has a sinful, unbelieving heart that turns away from the living God. ¹³But encourage one another daily, as long as it is called Today, so that none of you may be hardened by sin's deceitfulness. ¹⁴We have come to share in

Christ if we hold firmly till the end the confidence we had at first. *[15]As has just been said:*

> *"Today, if you hear his voice,*
> *do not harden your hearts*
> *as you did in the rebellion."*

[16]Who were they who heard and rebelled? Were they not all those who Moses led out of Egypt? [17]And with whom was he angry for forty years? Was it not those who sinned, whose bodies fell in the desert? [18]And to whom did God swear that they would never enter his rest if not to those who disobeyed? [19]So we see that they were not able to enter, because of their unbelief.

Hebrews 3:1–19

QUESTIONS FOR INTERACTION

LEADER

Refer to the Summary and Study Notes at the end of this session as needed. If 30 minutes is not enough time to answer all of the questions in this section, conclude the Bible Study by answering question #7.

1. Why does the author say that Jesus is worthy of greater honor than Moses? Why might it be important to make that point to those who were raised in the faith of Judaism?

2. What experience in the history of the Hebrew people are the readers urged not to repeat? What does it mean to "harden your heart" (vv. 8,15)?

3. Who are you most likely to harden your own heart against?
   ❐ The voice of the needy.
   ❐ The teaching of my parents.
   ❐ The Word of God.
   ❐ A loved one who has failed me.
   ❐ Other _____.

4. What does the author say is an important defense against "sin's deceitfulness" (v. 13)? When have you found this defense to be especially effective?

5. What does the author say we need to do in order to "share in Christ" (v. 14)? Why would it be important to say this in light of what the readers were facing?

6. What is the closest you have come to "turning away from the living God" (v. 12)? What were you going through at the time?

7. We are called to "encourage one another daily" (v. 13). In what area of your life are you especially needing encouragement right now?

GOING DEEPER: *If your group has time and/or wants a challenge, go on to this question.*

8. How does sin's deceitfulness "harden" us (v. 13)? In what ways does sin masquerade as something less destructive?

CARING TIME   15 Min.
APPLY THE LESSON AND PRAY FOR ONE ANOTHER

LEADER

Begin the Caring Time by having group members take turns sharing responses to all three questions. Be sure to save at least the last five minutes for a time of group prayer. Remember to include a prayer for the empty chair when concluding the prayer time.

Encouraging and supporting each other is especially vital if this group is to become all it can be. Take time now to "share in Christ" and pray for one another.

1. How is your relationship with Jesus right now?
- ❏ Close.
- ❏ Distant.
- ❏ Improving.
- ❏ Strained.
- ❏ Other _____.

2. How has this group been an encouragement to you? How can you help each other not to be hardened by sin's deceitfulness?

3. Remember to include in your prayers the encouragement people spoke of needing in question #7 under the Questions for Interaction.

NEXT WEEK

This week we discussed how rebelling against the Son is far worse than rebelling against Moses. We saw the consequences of unbelief and the hardening of the heart that can occur due to sin. In the coming week, make it a point to examine your conscience at the end of each day and confess your sins to God. Next week, we will see how the author takes a more positive approach by talking about the rewards in which we will share if we remain true to Christ.

NOTES on Hebrews 3:1–19

Summary: The author of Hebrews has already argued that Jesus is superior to the prophets (1:1–2), and the angels (1:3–2:13). Now he seeks to show that Jesus has a higher status than Moses. That would be even more outrageous than elevating a current political leader over George Washington or Abraham Lincoln. No wonder many Jews of the time were shocked at first by Christian teaching! Once the author has made this audacious statement, he goes on to say that the people should be wary of repeating the rebellion that occurred under Moses. The original Scripture reference to this rebellion is Exodus 17:1–7. However, the quote in verses 7–11 is from Psalm 95:7–11. This reminds us that even though the Jews of Jesus' day revered Moses, the people of Moses' own time rebelled against him. People so often reject the prophets of their own time and revere those of the past! Perhaps it is easier to apply scriptural truth to actions that are far removed from us, and which apply to people now dead, than it is to apply them to what we are currently doing. But God's Word will never be a living thing for us if we do that. We will forever be "hardening our hearts" to the direction of the Spirit, while thinking we are "religious" because we know what God used to do and what God said to people long ago.

The readers of this book were being tempted to turn back to this old way of dealing with God's Word. They were being tempted to harden their hearts to the personal meaning of God's Word for them. Hearing God's Word and seeing God's presence in the present time takes faith and courage, especially since there are always those (like the Pharisees were for Jesus) who will never be able to see beyond what was in the past. In light of such pressures, Christians were urged to encourage each other (v. 13). Such encouragement from one another helps us to hold fast to the Word that has been revealed to us.

3:1 Two phrases are used to remind the readers of who they are in Christ. ***holy brothers.*** This first phrase does not mean they are morally perfect, but that they have been "set apart" by God as his people. Today the word "holy" makes people feel uncomfortable and connotes a "holier than thou" or self-righteous attitude. But as Christians we should be holy in the sense of being dedicated to God. The word "brothers" is also important because it reminds us that we are not alone in whatever we face, but that we are part of a family. Since these readers were facing the possibility of persecution, it was important that they faced it together as a family. ***who share in the heavenly calling.*** This second phrase reminds the readers that they share in God's call and have special responsibilities toward God and one another. Popular thinking is that only the clergy have a calling from God, but that is not biblical. All of us have a calling to be used by God in some way to advance his kingdom. ***fix your thoughts.*** This implies concentrated attention and reflection. While Jesus helps believers deal with temptations, they are to focus their attention on him such that they will not be distracted by temptations to follow another course (12:2). ***the apostle.*** One who is sent with the full authority of the one who sent him or her (John 1:18).

3:3–6 Two analogies substantiate the claim that Jesus is worthy of far more honor than even Moses: (1) In terms of a house (or dynasty), Jesus is the builder (1:2) whereas Moses is part of the house itself; and (2) Moses was faithful as a *servant*, but Jesus is the *son* who owns the estate.

3:3 *worthy of greater honor than Moses.* Saying this would have been bordering on blasphemy for most Jewish people of the time! One second-century Jewish teacher, Rabbi Jose ben Chalafta said, "God calls Moses faithful in all his house, and thereby he ranked him higher than the ministering angels themselves."

3:6 *we are his house.* Some refer to a church building as God's "house," but Scripture more readily refers to God's people as God's "house" (1 Cor. 3:10–17; Eph. 2:19–22). This concept was very important for Jewish Christians. To meet God they no longer had to travel to a building, the temple, to find God's house—it could be found anywhere that God's people were. ***courage.*** Literally, "confidence." ***the hope.*** This is not a wish, but an expectation that is guaranteed to come about.

3:7–11 The psalmist recalls in Psalm 95:1–11 how the Israelites rebelled against both the Law and the mercies of God and thus never inherited the promise for which they had been delivered from Egypt. The Hebrew text of the psalm shows that Exodus 17:1–7 is in view, although its last verse points to Numbers 14:22–30.

3:11 *my rest.* In the context of the Israelites, this meant the promised land of Canaan where they would have prosperity and peace. For the readers of Hebrews it would mean the rest of God's eternal kingdom. In any case "rest" does not mean lying down or sleeping all of the time, but a sense of peace and contentment, such as one has after fulfilling a purpose. As God "rested" on the seventh day, so we shall have this rest of fulfillment.

3:12 *turns away.* Literally, "apostatizes." Whereas the warning in 2:1 was against "drifting" from the Lord, the concern here is a deliberate turning from God's way.

3:16–19 Through five questions based on events in Numbers 14:26–35, the author hammers home the importance of maintaining faith. Like the Israelites, these people will fail to inherit the fullness of life in Christ if they give in to unbelief.

SESSION 4
THE REST THAT GOD OFFERS

SCRIPTURE   HEBREWS 4:1–13

LAST WEEK

In our last session we were warned about the ultimate consequences for those who rebel against the Son. We were reminded to encourage one another to have faith and not lose heart in this world full of trials and temptations. In this session we will look at the reward for those who obey—a spiritual rest in the kingdom of God. This rest is available only to those who believe, and don't turn their back on that belief.

ICE-BREAKER   15 Min.
CONNECT WITH YOUR GROUP

- -

LEADER

Choose one, two or all three of the Ice-Breaker questions. Welcome and introduce new group members.

Deadlines, appointments, demands, a growing "to do" list—we live in a day where people feel a great deal of pressure. Share with the group how you have dealt with the pressures of everyday life.

1.   What do you most enjoy doing for relaxation? Would you describe your present status as well-rested, needing a break or totally exhausted?

2.   When you were a child and you were in trouble, where would you go to hide from your parents?

3.   Who is it that helps you to "cut to the heart of the matter" when you are facing a complicated decision?

BIBLE STUDY

READ SCRIPTURE AND DISCUSS

30 Min.

LEADER

Have a member of the group, selected ahead of time, read aloud the Scripture passage. Then discuss the Questions for Interaction, dividing into smaller subgroups of four or five.

Even God needed to rest on the seventh day after working for six days on the creation of the world! In today's Scripture passage, the author of Hebrews helps us to see what it means to join him in that rest when our work on this earth is through. Read Hebrews 4:1–13 and note the importance of faith and the promise of God in entering that rest.

A Sabbath-Rest for the People of God

4 *Therefore, since the promise of entering his rest still stands, let us be careful that none of you be found to have fallen short of it. ²For we also have had the gospel preached to us, just as they did; but the message they heard was of no value to them, because those who heard did not combine it with faith. ³Now we who have believed enter that rest, just as God has said,*

> *"So I declared on oath in my anger,*
> *'They shall never enter my rest.' "*

And yet his work has been finished since the creation of the world. ⁴For somewhere he has spoken about the seventh day in these words: "And on the seventh day God rested from all his work." ⁵And again in the passage above he says, "They shall never enter my rest."

⁶It still remains that some will enter that rest, and those who formerly had the gospel preached to them did not go in, because of their disobedience. ⁷Therefore God again set a certain day, calling it Today, when a long time later he spoke through David, as was said before:

> *"Today, if you hear his voice,*
> *do not harden your hearts."*

⁸For if Joshua had given them rest, God would not have spoken later about another day. ⁹There remains, then, a Sabbath-rest for the people of God; ¹⁰for anyone who enters God's rest also rests from his own work, just as God did from his. ¹¹Let us, therefore, make every effort to enter that rest, so that no one will fall by following their example of disobedience.

¹²For the word of God is living and active. Sharper than any double-edged sword, it penetrates even to dividing soul and spirit, joints and marrow; it judges the thoughts and attitudes of the heart. ¹³Nothing in all creation is hidden from God's sight. Everything is uncovered and laid bare before the eyes of him to whom we must give account.

Hebrews 4:1–13

LEADER

Refer to the Summary and Study Notes at the end of this session as needed. If 30 minutes is not enough time to answer all of the questions in this section, conclude the Bible Study by answering question #7.

QUESTIONS FOR INTERACTION

1. What should we learn from the negative example of the people of Israel who were denied entrance to the Promised Land? What do we need to do to avoid their mistake (vv. 1–3)?

2. From what you see in this passage and the relevant notes at the end of this study, what does it mean to "enter God's rest"? What is the main requirement for entering it?

3. What does the author say to convince his readers that "entering God's rest" means more than simply entering the land of Canaan under Joshua?

4. What connection does God's Word (vv. 12–13) have to the point the author was making about entering God's rest? If we truly believe that "everything is uncovered and laid bare" before God (v. 13), what effect does it have on our obedience (v. 11)?

5. Name four key words that the author uses to describe the Word of God. Choose one of them and share what insight it gives you into the nature of God's Word.

6. How do you feel about the fact that your actions are not hidden before God? Would it change your behavior at all if you remained constantly aware that God was watching you?

7. What dark area of your own life would you like for God's Word to penetrate, to help you better understand your own behavior?

GOING DEEPER: *If your group has time and/or wants a challenge, go on to this question.*

8. If indeed, "Nothing in all creation is hidden from God's sight" (v. 13), then why is it that there is so much injustice in the world? Are there some things God judges in this life, and some things only in the next?

CARING TIME   15 Min.

APPLY THE LESSON AND PRAY FOR ONE ANOTHER

LEADER

Be sure to save at least 15 minutes for this important time. After sharing responses to all three questions and asking for prayer requests, close in a time of group prayer.

Once again, take some time now to encourage one another in your faith by discussing the following questions and sharing prayer requests.

1. We can't hide from God, but we can hide from each other. How open and honest do you feel this group has been with each other to this point?

2. How are you doing at inviting people to fill "the empty chair"?

3. In what area of your life do you especially need some rest? How can the group help?

NEXT WEEK

Today we talked about the reward that awaits those who remain faithful and obedient to the message of the Gospel—a Sabbath-rest to be shared with God himself. That's a comforting thought to remember when the pressures of this world become overwhelming. In the coming week, take a few moments alone with God each day and just rest in his presence. Next week we will look at Jesus' role as "high priest," and how he helps us to share in that rest. We cannot get there on our own and Jesus is always there to show us the way.

NOTES ON HEBREWS 4:1–13

Summary: Entering God's rest and promised kingdom requires high standards; but, lest we despair, God gives us a superior resource to enable us to meet those standards. We will learn more about the resource to help us in our next session. For now, we will look at the high standards required for entering God's rest. Not just anyone can enter. The Israelites under Moses did not. They failed because of their disobedience. The writer of Hebrews was warning his readers that if they acted like those Israelites, they too would fail. He was warning them because, due to the rising pressure of persecution, some were looking like they too might fall by the wayside. Others were trying to get by through deception—making it appear that they were obedient, when in fact they were not. Many today also try that approach. But the writer points out to these people that nothing is hidden from God and his Word, which penetrates to the heart of all deceptions. We must give account to a God who sees all that we are and all that we do.

When we talk about God seeing and knowing all, some people, in the spirit of the rebellious child, only think about the fact that they can't get away with anything. However, there is another, more positive aspect in this. That we cannot hide from God can be reassuring once we understand that God loves us and wants the best for us. If we cannot hide from him, then we realize that we cannot subvert our own ultimate well-being by trying to run away. A dog can run away from its master and run into the street and be killed. We also can run away to our own destruction. God's ability to see and know all helps him keep us from such self-destructive behavior.

4:1 *the promise.* God's promise was to bring Israel into a "good and spacious land" where they would have peace (Ex. 3:8). However, the generation who originally received this promise never experienced its fulfillment. ***his rest.*** Rest is not a state of idleness but a condition in which one is free to live in peace, joy, security and freedom. Israel thought of rest in terms of dwelling securely in their own land, in freedom and prosperity (Deut. 5:33; 8:6–9). Later on, this developed into the hope of an eternal kingdom under the wise, compassionate leadership of a Davidic king (Ezek. 34:24–31; Dan. 7:13–14). It is likely that at least some of the original readers thought of this rest in such national, physical terms (Acts 1:6). ***let us be careful.*** Literally, "let us fear."

4:2 *those who heard did not combine it with faith.* The Israelites' failure to embrace God's deliverance with trust and obedience meant it was of no value to them.

4:3 *his work has been finished since the creation of the world.* The rabbis of Jesus' day often argued from something's absence in Scripture. In Genesis 2:2–3, there is no mention of an evening on the seventh day, the day of God's rest, as was mentioned with days one through six. From this the rabbis argued that, while the other days came to an end, the day of God's rest had no ending, therefore the rest of God was forever. This meant that though his works were finished at the creation of the world, his rest remains open for others to enter it (v. 6).

4:8 *For if Joshua had given them rest.* Joshua eventually led the people into the Promised Land, but since the Psalm 95 passage, written long after Joshua, still speaks of a promised rest, it must be referring to something more—something Joshua did not give the people when he led them into that land. What it refers to is the rest of being part of God's eternal kingdom.

4:9 *Sabbath-rest.* This term, found only here in the New Testament, is a play on words since the Greek words for "sabbath" and "rest" sound alike. It identifies this rest with the traditional Jewish Sabbath rest, yet accents that this rest fulfills the reality, which that one symbolized. Once again Jesus' superiority over all elements of traditional Jewish faith is emphasized. *the people of God.* This includes all people, Jew or Gentile, who entrust themselves to Jesus.

4:11 *make every effort.* Literally, "strive." The life of faith is not a passive waiting for God, but an urgent, determined resolve to push on in the pursuit of God.

4:12 *the word of God is living and active.* The Word of God is not a dead thing from the past, but a living thing with present application and relevance. But even more, it gets past the facades we present, cutting to the heart of who we are. We often try to hide ourselves from others, and sometimes we even try to do that before God, as Jonah did. But we cannot. God sends his word to confront us and keep us from hiding from him. The message here is similar to what we find in Psalm 139:7–12. *Sharper than any double-edged sword.* Isaiah made the first comparison of God's Word to a sword (Isa. 49:2). This demonstrates the piercing, discerning power of God's Word to cut through people's thoughts, intentions and motivations (Eph. 6:17; Rev. 1:16). *dividing soul and spirit ... thoughts and attitudes of the heart.* All of humanity—spirit, body and mind (the heart was referred to as the source of one's thought processes), is spoken to by God's Word.

4:13 *laid bare.* Three possibilities exist as to the meaning of this graphic image. It may refer to: (1) a wrestler whose head has been thrust back rendering him vulnerable to being pinned; (2) a soldier without armor to cover his throat; (3) a sacrificial animal whose neck is bared so that a knife can be drawn across its throat. All three images portray a frightening picture of being defenseless before an opponent.

THE GREAT HIGH PRIEST

SCRIPTURE HEBREWS 4:14–5:10

LAST WEEK

In last week's Scripture passage we were given hope that some day we will enter God's rest and be free from the pressures of this world, if we persevere in faith and obedience. This week we will look at how Jesus the Son of God helps us to be part of that rest by serving as a "high priest" between God the Father and us.

ICE-BREAKER   15 Min.
CONNECT WITH YOUR GROUP

LEADER

To help new group members get acquainted, remember to do all three Ice-Breaker questions.

"No man [or woman] is an island," has been a popular saying through the years to demonstrate that we all need each other's help to get through this life. Where we want to go is heaven, Jesus is the one who helps us get there. But who has helped you get to the point where you are right now, and what have been some high points of that journey? Take turns sharing your unique life experiences with the others in your group.

1. When you were a teenager, who best understood what you were going through and could empathize with you?

2. When you were a teenager, who, besides your actual father, was like a father to you? What did he do to guide and support you?

3. At this point in your life, what do you consider to be the greatest honor that has been conferred upon you?

BIBLE STUDY
READ SCRIPTURE AND DISCUSS

30 Min.

It always helps to have someone who knows what we are going through. In today's Scripture passage we will see how Jesus Christ knows that better than anyone because of what he went through in his earthly life. Read Hebrews 4:14–5:10 and note how Jesus serves as our high priest and our way to eternal life.

Jesus the Great High Priest

¹⁴*Therefore, since we have a great high priest who has gone through the heavens, Jesus the Son of God, let us hold firmly to the faith we profess.* ¹⁵*For we do not have a high priest who is unable to sympathize with our weaknesses, but we have one who has been tempted in every way, just as we are—yet was without sin.* ¹⁶*Let us then approach the throne of grace with confidence, so that we may receive mercy and find grace to help us in our time of need.*

5 *Every high priest is selected from among men and is appointed to represent them in matters related to God, to offer gifts and sacrifices for sins.* ²*He is able to deal gently with those who are ignorant and are going astray, since he himself is subject to weakness.* ³*This is why he has to offer sacrifices for his own sins, as well as for the sins of the people.*

⁴*No one takes this honor upon himself; he must be called by God, just as Aaron was.* ⁵*So Christ also did not take upon himself the glory of becoming a high priest. But God said to him,*

> *"You are my Son;*
> *today I have become your Father."*

⁶*And he says in another place,*

> *"You are a priest forever*
> *in the order of Melchizedek."* — appointed

⁷*During the days of Jesus' life on earth, he offered up prayers and petitions with loud cries and tears to the one who could save him from death, and he was heard because of his reverent submission.* ⁸*Although he was a son, he learned obedience from what he suffered* ⁹*and, once made perfect, he became the source of eternal salvation for all who obey him* ¹⁰*and was designated by God to be high priest in the order of Melchizedek.*

Hebrews 4:14–5:10

[handwritten: negated belief of 2 Messiahs - priest - king]

[handwritten: intense]

[handwritten: Jesus all man: body, soul, spirit]

[handwritten: not moral; perfect for the role hp & savior]

QUESTIONS FOR INTERACTION

1. Because we have a high priest like Jesus Christ, what should we be doing (4:14)? Why is this a natural response to having such a high priest?

2. Why is it important that Jesus was "tempted in every way, just as we are" (4:15)? Why is it important that in spite of these temptations he remained "without sin"?

3. What does it mean to you to "approach the throne of grace with confidence" (4:16)? What should this confidence be based on—belief in our own natural goodness, or faith in God's grace?

4. What do most high priests have to do that Jesus did not have to do (5:3; see also 4:15)?

5. What experience in Jesus' earthly life does verse 7 bring to mind for you? What does it mean to you that Jesus prayed to God "with loud cries and tears" (5:7)?

6. When do you remember praying to God "with loud cries and tears"—with all the feelings that were within you? Were you praying by yourself or with others? How did you feel about God's response to your prayers?

7. What temptation are you struggling with right now that you can't imagine Jesus having to face? If indeed Jesus "has been tempted in every way" just as you are, how does that understanding affect how you deal with your temptations?

GOING DEEPER: *If your group has time and/or wants a challenge, go on to this question.*

8. Why did Christ have to suffer in order to be perfect and to be "the source of eternal salvation for all who obey him" (5:9; see also 2:10)?

How does the torn curtain point us to the Great High Priest? what significance *impact* does this have on our every day lives?

'knowing Jesus as our HP

CARING TIME   15 Min.

APPLY THE LESSON AND PRAY FOR ONE ANOTHER

LEADER

Encourage everyone to participate in this important time and be sure that each group member is receiving prayer support. Continue to pray for the empty chair in the closing group prayer.

Even as Christ understands what we are going through, it helps to have other Christians who understand as well. This time of support and encouragement is an opportunity to do just that. Begin by sharing your responses to the questions below. Conclude by sharing prayer requests and praying for each other's needs.

1. What problem or trial do you need to pray about with more confidence, remembering that Jesus understands what you are going through?

2. What help do you need from Jesus right now to deal with your temptations?

3. How could you encourage and strengthen a brother or sister in Christ in the coming week?

NEXT WEEK

This week we sought to gain a better appreciation for Jesus' role as high priest. We were reminded that Jesus understands us and is always there to help us persevere in our faith. In the coming week, begin a daily prayer journal and keep track of prayer requests and answers. As you do this, your confidence will grow in approaching the throne of grace. Next week the author warns against wasting all of what Christ has done as high priest by turning away from the faith. We will learn the importance of not turning back and not "resting on our laurels" but keeping on in the quest to inherit what has been promised to us.

NOTES ON HEBREWS 4:14–5:10

Summary: In the last session we looked at the high standards required to enter God's rest. In today's Scripture passage, the author of Hebrews assures us that we have all the help we need in meeting these standards. We have a "great high priest"—Jesus Christ! That great high priest helps us to meet God's standards in two ways. First, as a high priest, he offered the sacrifice of himself to pay the penalty for our sin. Because of that we receive mercy and grace to help us (4:16). Second, it is equally true that this high priest understands what it is like to be tempted. In his earthly life he was tempted in all ways just as we are. This gives him empathy for us when we find ourselves to be weak and struggling. He knows what it is like to offer up prayers to God in the midst of tears. When we come to him in our weakened spiritual condition, he will understand and give us strength, as well as forgive us when we fall. Because he suffered as a human, and yet was divine and sinless, he became the perfect sacrifice for our sin and the source of our salvation.

4:14 *a great high priest.* The high priest served as the spiritual (and oftentimes civil) leader of the Jews. His most unique function was to bring a sacrifice to God in the Most Holy Place on the Day of Atonement.

4:15 *tempted in every way.* Jesus Christ came to this life to experience all the things that we experience as human beings. This does not mean that he tolerates our sin and weakness, or that he lets us get by with excuses. What it means is that he truly understands. This is what makes the fact that he knows us completely such good news. Jesus went through every kind of temptation we go through, and yet was without sin. There is no spiritual struggle we can take to him that he does not understand.

4:16 *approach ... with confidence.* If we were approaching God on our own merit, we would be scared and unsure because of our knowledge of our guilt. But since we know we are approaching the throne of grace, we can approach with boldness, believing God will accept us.

5:2 *since he himself is subject to weakness.* The most effective way to help another person going through a difficult time is often to empathize with them out of your own experiences of failure and pain.

5:5–6 The author may have used these two Old Testament texts to prove to some Jewish sects that the hope for the coming of two Messiahs (a kingly Messiah from David's line and a priestly Messiah from Aaron's line) is fulfilled in the one person of Jesus, the God-appointed priest and king. Psalm 2:7 and Psalm 110:4 are linked to show that Jesus' call to the priesthood can be traced to the mysterious Old Testament figure of Melchizedek, a king/priest who lived long before Aaron was born (Gen. 14:18–19). This connection between the Messiah and Melchizedek was unique to this author: it has no parallels in either Jewish or Christian thought of the time.

5:7 *prayers and petitions.* The two words overlap, but the latter most often indicates an intense pleading. ***loud cries and tears.*** Western culture does not typically associate such emotions with prayer, but this would be a normal part of sincere intercession by the faithful Jew. Jesus' prayer in Gethsemane may be in view (Matt. 26: 36–42). **and he was heard.** In one sense Jesus was not "saved from death." He had to pass through it to experience resurrection. The readers' experience may well be similar. **reverent submission.** Literally, "his godly fear." This is that awe before God that shaped the lives of the Old Testament saints who lived in the "fear of the Lord." As shown most clearly in his acceptance of the Cross, Jesus lived in complete accord with God's will.

5:8 *he learned obedience.* Even Jesus had to learn. He did not come forth from the womb as an all-knowing being. The necessity of his learning is doubtless why God provided even him with earthly parents.

5:9 *once made perfect.* This does not refer to moral perfection, but rather being made perfect for the role he was to fill—the perfect mediator. It is his sharing in the human experience of suffering that allows Jesus, the divine Son, to be fully capable of serving as intercessor for humanity.

SESSION 6
A WARNING AGAINST FALLING AWAY

SCRIPTURE HEBREWS 5:11–6:12

LAST WEEK

We learned to appreciate what it means to have Jesus as our "high priest" and the source of our salvation in last week's session. We were also reminded that Jesus understands our trials and temptations in this world and can help us get through them. In gratitude for all Jesus Christ has done for us, we need to be careful to hold onto our faith and not turn away from him. If we do turn away, his incredible sacrifice will have been in vain and we will once again be liable to condemnation. That is what today's passage in Hebrews warns us against.

ICE-BREAKER   15 Min.
CONNECT WITH YOUR GROUP

LEADER

Choose one or two of the Ice-Breaker questions. If you have a new group member you may want to do all three. Remember to stick closely to the three-part agenda and the time allowed for each segment.

Those who challenge themselves and achieve great things inspire us all. Our passage today is about growing beyond the basics so we are ready to weather the challenges of this life. What are the "basics" for you right now, and how are you doing at growing beyond them? Take turns sharing your experiences with maturing and learning.

1. In what areas of life do you need some "remedial learning"? In what areas do you feel like you have learned so much that you could teach others?

2. What foods do you consider to be the basics of your diet right now? If there were one food you would never want to do without, what would it be?

3. If you were to describe your life right now as a piece of land, what kind of land would it be?

❏ Fertile farmland.

❏ Rugged mountain terrain.

❏ A lawn with a mixture of grass, flowers and weeds.

❏ Arid desert.

❏ Other _____.

BIBLE STUDY   30 Min.
READ SCRIPTURE AND DISCUSS

LEADER

Select five members of the group ahead of time to read aloud the Scripture passage. Have each member read one paragraph, as outlined in the following Scripture reading. Then have the group divide into subgroups of four or five to discuss the Questions for Interaction.

Today's passage is somewhat of an aside from the author of Hebrews to his readers. He interrupts what he is telling them to chastise them for not growing at the rate at which they ought to be growing. Those who don't move forward are in danger of falling back! He wants to warn them against this, even though he assures them that he is confident of better things for them. Read Hebrews 5:11–6:12 and note what happens to those who have been enlightened, but then turn away from their faith.

Warning Against Falling Away

Reader 1:   ¹¹*We have much to say about this, but it is hard to explain because you are slow to learn. ¹²In fact, though by this time you ought to be teachers, you need someone to teach you the elementary truths of God's word all over again. You need milk, not solid food! ¹³Anyone who lives on milk, being still an infant, is not acquainted with the teaching about righteousness. ¹⁴But solid food is for the mature, who by constant use have trained themselves to distinguish good from evil.*

Reader 2:   *6Therefore let us leave the elementary teachings about Christ and go on to maturity, not laying again the foundation of repentance from acts that lead to death, and of faith in God, ²instruction about baptisms, the laying on of hands, the resurrection of the dead, and eternal judgment. ³And God permitting, we will do so.*

Reader 3:   ⁴*It is impossible for those who have once been enlightened, who have tasted the heavenly gift, who have shared in the Holy Spirit, ⁵who have tasted the goodness of the word of God and the powers of the coming* *age, ⁶if they fall away, to be brought back to repentance, because to their loss they are crucifying the Son of God all over again and subjecting him to public disgrace.*

Reader 4: *⁷Land that drinks in the rain often falling on it and that produces a crop useful to those for whom it is farmed receives the blessing of God. ⁸But land that produces thorns and thistles is worthless and is in danger of being cursed. In the end it will be burned.*

Reader 5: *⁹Even though we speak like this, dear friends, we are confident of better things in your case—things that accompany salvation. ¹⁰God is not unjust; he will not forget your work and the love you have shown him as you have helped his people and continue to help them. ¹¹We want each of you to show this same diligence to the very end, in order to make your hope sure. ¹²We do not want you to become lazy, but to imitate those who through faith and patience inherit what has been promised.*

Hebrews 5:11–6:12

QUESTIONS FOR INTERACTION

LEADER

Refer to the Summary and Study Notes at the end of this session as needed. If 30 minutes is not enough time to answer all of the questions in this section, conclude the Bible Study by answering question #7.

1. How would you describe the author's approach in dealing with his readers in this passage?
    ❒ Overly sarcastic.
    ❒ Challenging.
    ❒ Judgmental.
    ❒ Tough, but fair.
    ❒ Impatient.
    ❒ Positive in the end.

2. What was the author saying when he wrote that his readers needed "milk, not solid food" (5:12)? What might be some examples of Christian teaching that is "milk"? What might be some examples of some "solid food" issues? Do Christians always need a certain amount of "milk" (see also 1 Peter 2:2)?

3. What does the author consider to be elementary, foundational teachings (6:1–2)?

4. The author contends that if a person turns away after experiencing five aspects of Christian faith, they cannot be "brought back to repentance" (6:6). What are those five aspects of the faith?

5. What does a person do to Christ when he or she falls away from the faith?

6. On what does the author base his confidence that the readers will not fall away in the manner he has described? What does he say God will not forget?

7. When in your life have you been closest to falling away from your faith? What happened to cause this time of spiritual stress? If you are through that time now, what helped you through it? If you are not through that time, where are you looking for help?

GOING DEEPER: *If your group has time and/or wants a challenge, go on to this question.*

8. What causes people to fall away from Christian faith? What can Christians do to best support people in this time? Does it help more to threaten them with loss of salvation (6:4–8), or to take a more positive, supportive approach (6:9–12)?

CARING TIME   15 Min.
APPLY THE LESSON AND PRAY FOR ONE ANOTHER

....

Help each other to grow in faith from "milk" to "solid food" by encouraging and supporting one another with a time of sharing and prayer.

1. What season are you experiencing in your spiritual life right now?
❑ The warmth of summer.
❑ The dead of winter.
❑ The new life of spring.
❑ The changes of fall.

2. Where are you seeing some "thorns and thistles" in your life that you need some help in weeding out?

3. Take time to focus on each member of your group and affirm one area where you see that person "producing a useful crop" in his or her Christian growth.

Today we were warned against falling away from the beautiful faith that Jesus, through his sacrificial suffering and death, won for us. We were cautioned about feeding ourselves only with "milk" (elementary truths of God's Word), instead of moving on to "solid food" and becoming teachers rather than students. In the coming week, take some time to study an issue of faith that you struggle with. Next week we will feast on some "solid food" as we consider one of the truly mysterious figures in Scripture—Melchizedek. We will consider how Christ is like him and what that means to our faith journey.

NOTES ON HEBREWS 5:11–6:12

Summary: This is the first section of Hebrews that indicates this might be a letter addressed to a specific group of people. Everything else written to this point could be considered a general treatise to the church at large. The writer had been dealing with some pretty heady matters—the nature of the priesthood and the relationship of Christ to all that had gone before in the faith of Israel. He now stops to consider whether he may be trying to teach some things that are beyond the readers' grasp. He insists that such things shouldn't be too hard for them. They had been Christians for some time, and in fact ought to be teachers themselves (5:12). But they seemed to be content dealing with only the elementary "milk" issues of the faith. The writer now tells them that they must progress beyond such issues. Part of the reason that they must progress beyond such elementary issues is due to the increased likelihood of falling away from the faith. It was like he was saying, "If you're not moving forward, you are in danger of falling back." There is no standing still in life, especially in the Christian faith. Jesus had said, "No one who puts his hand to the plow and looks back is fit for service in the kingdom of God" (Luke 9:62). In more recent times, Bob Dylan said, "He who is not busy being born is busy dying." That is what this passage is about.

5:12 *though by this time.* The readers of this letter have apparently been Christians for some time. They were not new in the faith. ***milk/solid food.*** Milk is the basic teaching you would expect to give to seekers or new Christians. Solid food refers to the difficult truths that mature Christians struggle to understand (1 Cor. 3:1–3; 1 Peter 2:1–3).

5:14 *by constant use have trained themselves.* Spiritual maturity, like emotional maturity, is developed through practicing healthy disciplines over a period of time—disciplines like prayer, worship, devotion and good works (1 Cor. 9:24–27).

6:2 *not laying again the foundation.* This does not mean abandoning such teaching, but rather taking a step beyond it. It is basic teaching about Christ that is at the foundation of it all (1 Cor. 3:11). However, once the foundation is laid, you don't go back and lay it over and over again. You move on to issues and understandings that will make you more mature. These teachings were what the author saw as foundational: (1) repentance from acts that lead to death (Rom. 5:12–13); (2) faith in God; (3) instruction about baptisms—baptism included instruction as to what it meant; (4) laying on of hands—this was the way the Holy Spirit was conveyed; (5) the resurrection of the dead—Paul says this is pivotal for the faith (1 Cor 15:12–19); and (6) eternal judgment. While all of these were Christian basics, all also could be found in Judaism, and the readers may have lost sight of how Jesus had changed their meaning.

6:4–6 *impossible ... to be brought back to repentance.* The meaning of this phrase is much debated. Some have interpreted it to mean that there is no forgiveness for deliberate sin after baptism. Others have thought it refers to those who have "come forward" at a worship service to make a decision for Christ, but then, after the emotion has subsided, have had second thoughts. *those who have once been enlightened.* Being enlightened was seen as an equivalent to repenting and being baptized. *have tasted the heavenly gift.* Here the author affirms Paul's teaching that salvation is a gift of God's grace. "Tasted" is a sensual term that the author repeats again in verse 5. The person being described, then, is one who has gone beyond a shallow, superficial, emotional decision to a fuller experience of salvation. *shared in the Holy Spirit.* Again this indicates that the person has made more than a whimsical decision that has gone away when the emotion subsided. *have tasted the goodness of the word of God.* The person has found by experience how fol-

lowing God's Word can bring fullness and meaning to life. *and the powers of the coming age.* The powers the disciples had to heal, speak in tongues and cast out demons were seen as powers that foreshadowed the coming culmination of God's kingdom. This was a time when persecution was mounting in the church, and the possibility that some might deny their faith was great. If a person would do such a thing, after knowing all that Christ offers, it would be like they were crucifying Christ again.

6:7–8 This is reminiscent of Jesus' Parable of the Sower, or as it is also called, the Parable of the Soils. God blesses land that produces usable crops in response to rain, but land that responds with only weeds is likely to be cursed (by the farmer if not by God!). Those who respond to God's grace with disobedience are in danger of God's judgment.

6:9 *we are confident of better things.* The author now seeks to take a positive approach. Obviously since he was mentioning these things in his letter, and since he already had said that they were not ready to go on to the more mature things he wanted to talk about, he felt what he was saying about falling away could apply to some of them. However, perhaps the author had a sense of modern psychology, which sees positive affirmation as a better motivator than negative criticism.

6:10 *he will not forget your work.* God will not overlook the things that they are doing right and judge them only on what they have done wrong.

6:11 *show this same diligence to the very end.* This is the "bottom line" for the author. Leading the Christian life takes diligence. We are never at a place where we should think that we can just "coast" on in.

A PRIEST LIKE MELCHIZEDEK

SCRIPTURE   HEBREWS 7:11–28

LAST WEEK

We must continue growing and maturing in our faith, or we may be in danger of losing that precious faith. Last week the author reminded us of this by emphasizing the importance of moving beyond "milk" issues and challenging ourselves with some "solid food." This week he truly does that as he introduces the figure of Melchizedek, a king and priest who lived during the time of Abraham. Melchizedek received priestly authority through special divine selection rather than descent, and foreshadowed Christ in many ways.

ICE-BREAKER   15 Min.
CONNECT WITH YOUR GROUP

LEADER

Introduce and welcome new group members. If there are no new members, choose one or two of the Ice-Breaker questions to get started. If there are new members, then discuss all three.

Before we delve into the past to talk of Melchizedek, let's delve into our own pasts and discover what treasures are there. Take turns sharing your experiences and history with one another.

1. What nation did your ancestors come from? Is there anything in particular that people of this nationality are known for?

2. What person from the past, real or fictional, would you most want to be like (excluding Jesus)? What about this person would you most want to emulate?

3. Who was most likely to intercede for you when you were a child?

BIBLE STUDY
READ SCRIPTURE AND DISCUSS

30 Min.

LEADER

Ask a member of the group, selected ahead of time, to read aloud the Scripture passage. Then discuss the Questions for Interaction, dividing into subgroups of four or five.

One method of describing someone is to comparing him or her to someone else who has similar characteristics. The author does that here by comparing Jesus to Melchizedek. This comparison may seem unusual to us, because we see Melchizedek as an obscure figure. However, the people of the time probably would have been much more familiar with him than we are. The author compares Christ to him in two areas: neither became priests on the basis of descent, and both had an "indestructible life" (v. 16). Read Hebrews 7:11–28 and note how Jesus is our perfect high priest.

Jesus Like Melchizedek

[11]*If perfection could have been attained through the Levitical priesthood (for on the basis of it the law was given to the people), why was there still need for another priest to come—one in the order of Melchizedek, not in the order of Aaron?* [12]*For when there is a change of the priesthood, there must also be a change of the law.* [13]*He of whom these things are said belonged to a different tribe, and no one from that tribe has ever served at the altar.* [14]*For it is clear that our Lord descended from Judah, and in regard to that tribe Moses said nothing about priests.* [15]*And what we have said is even more clear if another priest like Melchizedek appears,* [16]*one who has become a priest not on the basis of a regulation as to his ancestry but on the basis of the power of an indestructible life.* [17]*For it is declared:*

"You are a priest forever,
in the order of Melchizedek."

[18]*The former regulation is set aside because it was weak and useless* [19]*(for the law made nothing perfect), and a better hope is introduced, by which we draw near to God.*

[20]*And it was not without an oath! Others became priests without any oath,* [21]*but he became a priest with an oath when God said to him:*

"The Lord has sworn
and will not change his mind:
'You are a priest forever.' "

[22]*Because of this oath, Jesus has become the guarantee of a better covenant.*

[23]*Now there have been many of those priests, since death pre-*

vented them from continuing in office; ²⁴but because Jesus lives forever, he has a permanent priesthood. ²⁵Therefore he is able to save completely those who come to God through him, because he always lives to intercede for them.

²⁶Such a high priest meets our need—one who is holy, blameless, pure, set apart from sinners, exalted above the heavens. ²⁷Unlike the other high priests, he does not need to offer sacrifices day after day, first for his own sins, and then for the sins of the people. He sacrificed for their sins once for all when he offered himself. ²⁸For the law appoints as high priests men who are weak; but the oath, which came after the law, appointed the Son, who has been made perfect forever.

Hebrews 7:11–28

QUESTIONS FOR INTERACTION

LEADER

Refer to the Summary and Study Notes at the end of this session as needed. If 30 minutes is not enough time to answer all of the questions in this section, conclude the Bible Study by answering question #7.

1. What argument does the author make to establish that the priests descended from Aaron were inadequate?

2. What tribe was Jesus descended from? Why does the author point out that this tribe had no ancestral association with the priesthood? If Christ has no ancestral claim to the priesthood, on what was his claim based? How is this like Melchizedek (see 7:1–10)?

3. How does the author describe "the former regulation" (the Old Testament Law)? What is the source of "a better hope" (vv. 18–19)?

4. What connection does the writer make between the old priesthood and the Old Testament Law (vv. 12,18–19)? What is Jesus' priesthood connected with (v. 22)?

5. How does the fact that Jesus conquered death through his resurrection affect his function as priest? Why does this help him "save completely" those who come to God through him (v. 25)?

6. What are the qualities Jesus has as high priest that help him meet our needs? Which of these qualities seems most important to you?

7. When a lawyer makes intercession for us in court, he or she first discusses our case with us and hears what we want to say that will help our defense. As Jesus prepares to intercede for you, what would you especially want to say to him?

GOING DEEPER: *If your group has time and/or wants a challenge, go on to this question.*

8. Why did Christ only have to make his sacrifice once, as opposed to the daily sacrifices other priests had to make? Why is a sacrifice necessary at all (9:22; Rom 6:23)?

CARING TIME   15 Min.

APPLY THE LESSON AND PRAY FOR ONE ANOTHER

LEADER

Continue to encourage group members to invite new people to the group. Remind everyone that this group is for learning and sharing, but also for reaching out to others. Close the group prayer by thanking God for each member and for this time together.

Take some time now to pray for one another, remembering that Jesus "always lives to intercede" for his people (v. 25). Begin by sharing your responses to the following questions. Then share prayer requests and close with prayer.

1. What was the high point of last week for you? What was the low point?

2. What is something that you would like to thank Jesus for doing for you as your eternal high priest?

3. On a scale of 1 (not at all) to 10 (completely fulfilled), how would you rate the way your spiritual needs are being met at this point in your life? How can this group help?

NEXT WEEK

Today we got an inspiring look at the nature of Christ's priesthood. We were comforted by the fact that Jesus can truly meet all of our needs and lives to constantly intercede on our behalf. In the coming week, pray daily for each member of the group and remember the prayer requests that were mentioned today. Next week we will continue to look at the beautiful nature of Christ's priesthood and what that means for the new covenant between God and us.

NOTES ON HEBREWS 7:11–28

Summary: For many students of the Bible, this section of Hebrews on Melchizedek is one of the strangest, most confusing passages in the New Testament. Who is this Melchizedek, really, and why is so much made of a man about whom the Old Testament says so little? While we may not be able to fully answer that question, remember that Melchizedek would not have been as obscure a figure to the original readers as he is to readers today. Christian writers did not invent him or initiate the focus on him. Also, it was a common rabbinical practice to assume that what is not written in Scripture didn't exist. So the fact that there was no reference to Melchizedek's father or mother, or birth or death, meant that he was without parents and had no beginning or end. That his name meant "king of righteousness" and that he was king of Salem, which meant "Peace," also provided a link to Jesus Christ (see 7:1–3).

In many respects what the author of Hebrews says about the priesthoods of Melchizedek and Jesus, in contrast to that of the Levitical priests, could be compared to the difference between leadership by virtue of one's position versus leadership by virtue of a charismatic personality. Who would you be more likely to follow in a crisis: the person who an authority figure has designated as leader, or the person who by his or her knowledge and strength of character shows that he or she can get done what needs to be done? Jesus' authority was not established by traditional methods, but came by virtue of what he accomplished—his victory over death itself (vv. 16,27).

7:11 *If perfection could have been attained.* Had the previous system of traditional Judaism been adequate, then the prophecies the author of Hebrews has been referring to (5:6; 6:20; 7:17), would not have talked about a different kind of priest to come. Something more and better is needed. The author makes similar statements in 4:8–9 about the inadequacy of the earthly Promised Land, and in 8:7 about the first covenant being inadequate.

7:12 *For when there is a change of the priesthood.* The priesthood was such an integral part of the Old Testament legal system that getting rid of it would have to imply that the whole system had to be overhauled.

7:14 *our Lord descended from Judah.* Jesus was referred to as a son of David, and David was of the tribe of Judah (Matt. 1:1–16; Luke 3:23–38). Priests were to be descendants of Aaron and assisted by men from the tribe of Levi (Num. 3:1–10; 8:5–26).

7:16–17 The Levitical priesthood was based solely on ancestry. The new priesthood is based on one's eternal nature. Jesus' resurrection thus qualified him to be the better high priest foretold in Psalm 110 (v. 17).

7:18–19 *perfect.* While the endless repetition of sacrifices served to remind people of their sin, it was powerless to change their condition (10:3–4; Rom. 3:20).

7:20–21 *oath.* The Levitical priests were appointed by divine command (Num. 8), but there was no oath involved. In contrast, as the full quote from Psalm 110:4 reveals, God's promise of a new high priest is sealed with an oath.

7:22 *guarantee.* This literally means "surety." Covenants were sealed with a pledge as a token that their terms would be carried out. Jesus' sacrifice is God's pledge for the new covenant. ***a better covenant.*** A covenant was a binding commitment of mutual obligations between two parties. In the case of ancient kings, covenants were unilateral in that the king determined what both he and his subjects would do for one another. This better covenant will be discussed more in chapter 8.

7:23–24 Naturally priests died, so their service was only temporary and they had to be replaced. Jesus' superior priesthood is evidenced by the fact that he lives forever.

7:25 *save completely.* One of Hebrew's main themes is that Jesus has the power to truly cleanse believers from sin and thus enable them to draw near to God (4:16; 6:19–20; 9:14; 10:19–22). Since the old priests were not invulnerable to death, they could never hope to save their people from life's one ultimate certainty. Jesus, who conquered death, thus has the ability to save believers from death itself. His eternal presence before God means believers are never without a representative in God's presence.

A NEW COVENANT

SCRIPTURE   HEBREWS 8:1–13

LAST WEEK

In last week's session we looked at what it means to have Jesus as our eternal high priest in heaven. We were joyfully reminded that he became the perfect sacrifice for our sin and he now lives to intercede for us and help us. Today we will consider what Jesus' priesthood implies for the nature of the new covenant he mediates. This covenant, predicted by the prophet Jeremiah, ushers in and establishes a deeper relationship between God and his people, and provides for complete forgiveness of sins.

ICE-BREAKER   15 Min.
CONNECT WITH YOUR GROUP

. . . .

LEADER

Choose one, two or all three of the Ice-Breaker questions. Be sure to welcome and introduce new group members.

The author of Hebrews speaks a lot about things on earth being built on a pattern or set of instructions from above. How do you do with patterns and instructions? Take turns sharing your experiences with your group.

1. Which of the following activities involving patterns did you enjoy doing as a child?
   ❏ Paint by number.
   ❏ Making model cars or airplanes.
   ❏ Making dresses or other clothes.
   ❏ Building with an Erector set.
   ❏ Other _____.

2. How good are you at following instructions?
   ❏ I can only follow the "for dummies" version.
   ❏ I only consult the instructions if all else fails.
   ❏ I do everything by the book, studying instructions thoroughly before beginning.
   ❏ Other _____.

3. In the family in which you were raised, did your parents pretty much legislate what you and your siblings were to do, or did you sometimes have "family meetings" where such things were discussed? Was there ever a chance to "renegotiate" responsibilities and privileges? How does this work in your present family?

BIBLE STUDY   30 Min.
READ SCRIPTURE AND DISCUSS

LEADER

Ask two members of the group, selected ahead of time, to read aloud the Scripture passage. Have one member read verses 1–8a and 13, and the other read verses 8b–12. Then have the group divide into subgroups of four or five to discuss the Questions for Interaction.

The fact that we have a high priest who is superior to the old priesthood system implies that the covenant this high priest ushers in is also superior to the old one. This new covenant will be written on our hearts and will provide for our forgiveness. Read Hebrews 8:1–13 and note all of the benefits of the new covenant.

The High Priest of a New Covenant

Reader 1:

8 *The point of what we are saying is this: We do have such a high priest, who sat down at the right hand of the throne of the Majesty in heaven, ²and who serves in the sanctuary, the true tabernacle set up by the Lord, not by man.*

³Every high priest is appointed to offer both gifts and sacrifices, and so it was necessary for this one also to have something to offer. ⁴If he were on earth, he would not be a priest, for there are already men who offer the gifts prescribed by the law. ⁵They serve at a sanctuary that is a copy and shadow of what is in heaven. This is why Moses was warned when he was about to build the tabernacle: "See to it that you make everything according to the pattern shown you on the mountain." ⁶But the ministry Jesus has received is as superior to theirs as the covenant of which he is mediator is superior to the old one, and it is founded on better promises.

⁷For if there had been nothing wrong with that first covenant, no place would have been sought for another. ⁸But God found fault with the people and said:

Reader 2:   *"The time is coming, declares the Lord,*
        when I will make a new covenant
    with the house of Israel
        and with the house of Judah.

> *⁹It will not be like the covenant*
> *I made with their forefathers*
> *when I took them by the hand*
> *to lead them out of Egypt,*
> *because they did not remain faithful to my covenant,*
> *and I turned away from them, declares the Lord.*
> *¹⁰This is the covenant I will make with the house of Israel*
> *after that time, declares the Lord.*
> *I will put my laws in their minds*
> *and write them on their hearts.*
> *I will be their God,*
> *and they will be my people.*
> *¹¹No longer will a man teach his neighbor,*
> *or a man his brother, saying, 'Know the Lord,'*
> *because they will all know me,*
> *from the least of them to the greatest.*
> *¹²For I will forgive their wickedness*
> *and will remember their sins no more."*

Reader 1:   *¹³By calling this covenant "new," he has made the first one obsolete; and what is obsolete and aging will soon disappear.*

Hebrews 8:1–13

QUESTIONS FOR INTERACTION

LEADER

Refer to the Summary and Study Notes at the end of this session as needed. If 30 minutes is not enough time to answer all of the questions in this section, conclude the Bible Study by answering question #7.

1. What makes the tabernacle Jesus serves in the "true" tabernacle? Where is it located?

2. How does the earthly tabernacle relate to the one in which Jesus now serves (v. 5)? What was Moses warned about building this tabernacle?

3. What does the author say demonstrates that there was something wrong with the old covenant?

4. How is the new covenant different from the old one, according to the prophecy quoted in verses 8–12?

5. What had the old law been written on (Ex. 31:18)? In contrast, where is this new law to be written? What does this imply about the nature of this law?

6. When has God "taken you by the hand" to lead you out of "Egypt"—a place or time when you felt enslaved?

7. What happened in your life to change your commitment to God from an obligation to a heartfelt love commitment? If this has not happened yet, what would need to happen in order for you to make this transition?

GOING DEEPER: *If your group has time and/or wants a challenge, go on to this question.*

8. If the old covenant is now "obsolete" as the author says, does that mean that Old Testament laws have no value or applicability to the Christian? What role should these laws have, if any, in our lives (Matt. 5:17–20; Rom. 7:1–20)?

CARING TIME   15 Min.
APPLY THE LESSON AND PRAY FOR ONE ANOTHER

LEADER

Have you started working with your group about their mission—perhaps by sharing the dream of multiplying into two groups by the end of this study of Hebrews?

Giving each other encouragement and support is one way we can be part of freeing each other from the "Egypts" of life, and finding a new and heartfelt relationship with God. Take turns sharing your responses to these questions before closing in prayer.

1. What's your biggest concern about next week?

2. How would you like to praise and thank God for deliverance from the "Egypts" of your life?

3. How can this group help you claim the promise that God will "remember your sins no more"?

NEXT WEEK

Today we learned of the new covenant mediated by Jesus Christ. This new covenant is superior to the old covenant and provides a way for a much more personal relationship with God. It also gives us the assurance that God will forgive and forget all of our sins. In the coming week, write down your sins on a piece of paper, confess them to God and then tear up the paper and throw it away, believing your sins are now forgiven. Next week we will see how Christ established this precious covenant with his own life and blood, which pays the price of our sin and brings us forgiveness.

NOTES ON HEBREWS 8:1–13

Summary: People today are familiar with the phrase, "renegotiating the contract." Most often we hear this phrase in connection with some high-priced athlete. The athlete has had a good season, or has heard of some rival who received a contract for more money than he or she makes, and now feels cheated. However, in Hebrews we hear of a different kind of renegotiated contract. In this case it is a renegotiation of the contract between God and humanity, and God, not a disgruntled humanity, initiates it. God saw that humanity was not living up to the old contract and, rather than simply writing us off, he introduced a new contract which gives us an important new benefit—grace. The one who brings this grace is the high priest who the author has been writing about in previous chapters, Jesus Christ the Son of God.

The previous contract had required that humanity be able to live up to a variety of laws that God had written in stone and handed to Moses on Mount Sinai. Because of the weakness of human sinfulness, we could not. Through the grace of God in Jesus Christ, the new contract calls for Jesus to pay the penalty demanded by the old (death), and for people to gain good standing before God through faith in this sacrifice, and allegiance to Christ as Lord. The end result is that for such a person God declares, "I will remember their sin no more."

8:2 *sanctuary.* This refers to the Most Holy Place in the temple (9:3). ***tabernacle.*** God gave Moses a pattern for how to build a copy of the true heavenly tabernacle (Ex. 26). Jesus' greatness is seen in that he serves in this true tabernacle, not in an earthly copy. The tabernacle, an elaborate movable tent, gave way to Solomon's Temple and, later still, to the Herodian Temple destroyed by the Romans in A.D. 70. The fact that the author does not refer to this destruction as proof that the old order had passed away (v. 13) is a strong clue that the letter was written prior to that date. The focus on the tabernacle may have been because some Jewish sects considered the current administration of the temple services to be corrupted and invalid. Greek-speaking Jews who lived far from Jerusalem likewise considered the temple largely irrelevant to their worship.

8:3 *gifts and sacrifices.* A primary function of the Old Testament high priests was to offer sacrifice on the Day of Atonement (Lev. 16). Jesus, as a priest, must likewise have a sacrifice to offer—namely, himself (7:27).

8:5 *copy and shadow.* These words communicate the difference between the physical, visible nature of the old covenant and the spiritual, heavenly nature of the new. They reflect what is essentially a Platonic philosophy that influenced the author. In this philosophy, everything in our earthly life is really just a copy or shadow of a higher reality. Levitical priests offer sacrifice in a sanctuary that is just a shadow of the true heavenly one, while Jesus serves as priest in the heavenly reality itself. The quote is from Exodus 25:40.

8:6 Jesus' ministry supersedes that of the old priests because the new covenant accomplishes that which the old never could (vv. 7–13). ***mediator.*** Since a covenant involved two parties, the mediator served as a go-between to work out the various terms of the covenant between the two parties making the covenant. **better promises.** The new covenant promises are "better" in that they promise far more than was ever promised in the old.

8:8–12 Jeremiah prophesied just prior to Babylon's conquest of Judah in 586 B.C. When the Jews were free to return to Jerusalem about 70 years later, expectations ran high that this prophecy was being fulfilled. Christians saw it fulfilled instead in the covenant established by Christ. The whole existence of what we call the Old and New Testament is based on this. A "testament" is another word for a covenant or agreement. So, the divisions of the Bible have to do with the difference between the old and the new agreement between God and humanity. The old agreement had faults, which was why it had to be replaced. Essentially, the problem was that it did not bring God and humanity together. This was because of human frailty, or as verse 9 says, "because they did not remain faithful to my covenant."

8:10 *I will put my laws in their minds and write them on their hearts.* This contrasts "internal" versus "external" motivation. Internal motivation is when we follow God's way because of the love for him in our heart. External motivation is when we follow God's way because we are afraid that if we don't, we will be punished. It is the former that the new covenant seeks to focus on. This requires nothing less than a change of heart, which comes by virtue of being in a trusting relationship with God through Jesus Christ (Gal. 2:20).

THE BLOOD OF CHRIST

SCRIPTURE   HEBREWS 9:11–28

LAST WEEK

Last week we looked at the new covenant that God has established with us in Jesus Christ. This new covenant brings us great hope and peace as it provides a way for God to forgive and forget our sins. During this session we will continue to learn more about the sacrifice that Christ made in order to establish the new covenant with his own life and blood. This sacrifice was given once for all of us, and the author appeals to us to be receptive to that gift.

ICE-BREAKER   15 Min.

CONNECT WITH YOUR GROUP

LEADER

Welcome and introduce new group members. Choose one, two or all three Ice-Breaker questions, depending on your group's needs.

Sometimes talking about blood and holy places seems a little foreign to us. But if we think about it, these things have had a place in our own past. Take turns sharing some of your unique life experiences with one another.

1. What was the closest thing to a "holy place" (strictly off-limits!) in the home where you were raised?
    ❑ Our parents' room.
    ❑ An older sibling's room.
    ❑ The living room (only when there are special guests!).
    ❑ A drawer or chest where mementos were kept.
    ❑ Other _____.

    Do you ever remember "violating" that holy place?

2. When you were a child, how did you most often react to the sight of your own blood? "Cool!"—or—"Help, Mom, I'm dying!"? What particularly bloody accident do you remember having as a child or adolescent?

3. Have you written your will? How did you feel about that experience? Was it something you had to be dragged to do "kicking and screaming," or did you pretty much do it on your own?

BIBLE STUDY

READ SCRIPTURE AND DISCUSS

30 Min.

LEADER

Select a member of the group ahead of time to read aloud the Scripture passage. Then discuss the Questions for Interaction, dividing into subgroups of four or five.

As our "high priest," Christ inaugurated a new covenant—a covenant that was put into effect through his own blood. Today's Scripture passage helps us to see how the shedding of Christ's blood was essential to the establishment of this new covenant between God and us. Read Hebrews 9:11–28 and note how the ultimate sacrifice that Christ made fulfilled all of the demands of the old covenant.

The Blood of Christ

[11]When Christ came as high priest of the good things that are already here, he went

through the greater and more perfect tabernacle that is not man-made, that is to say, not a part of this creation. [12]He did not enter by means of the blood of goats and calves; but he entered the Most Holy Place once for all by his own blood, having obtained eternal redemption. [13]The blood of goats and bulls and the ashes of a heifer sprinkled on those who are ceremonially unclean sanctify them so that they are outwardly clean. [14]How much more, then, will the blood of Christ, who through the eternal Spirit offered himself unblemished to God, cleanse our consciences from acts that lead to death, so that we may serve the living God!

[15]For this reason Christ is the mediator of a new covenant, that those who are called may receive the promised eternal inheritance—now that he has died as a ransom to set them free from the sins committed under the first covenant.

[16]In the case of a will, it is necessary to prove the death of the one who made it, [17]because a will is in force only when somebody has died; it never takes effect while the one who made it is living. [18]This is why even the first covenant was not put into effect without blood. [19]When Moses had proclaimed every commandment of the law to all the people, he took the blood of calves, together with water, scarlet wool and branches of hyssop, and sprinkled the scroll and all the people. [20]He said, "This is the blood of the covenant, which God has commanded you to keep." [21]In the same way, he sprinkled with the blood both the tabernacle and everything used in its ceremonies. [22]In fact, the law requires that nearly

everything be cleansed with blood, and without the shedding of blood there is no forgiveness.

²³It was necessary, then, for the copies of the heavenly things to be purified with these sacrifices, but the heavenly things themselves with better sacrifices than these. ²⁴For Christ did not enter a man-made sanctuary that was only a copy of the true one; he entered heaven itself, now to appear for us in God's presence. ²⁵Nor did he enter heaven to offer himself again and again, the way the high priest enters the Most Holy Place every year with blood that is not his own. ²⁶Then Christ would have had to suffer many times since the creation of the world. But now he has appeared once for all at the end of the ages to do away with sin by the sacrifice of himself. ²⁷Just as man is destined to die once, and after that to face judgment, ²⁸so Christ was sacrificed once to take away the sins of many people; and he will appear a second time, not to bear sin, but to bring salvation to those who are waiting for him.

Hebrews 9:11–28

QUESTIONS FOR INTERACTION

LEADER

Refer to the Summary and Study Notes at the end of this session as needed. If 30 minutes is not enough time to answer all of the questions in this section, conclude the Bible Study by answering question #8.

1. If you were to make a "spiritual will" where you could leave spiritual qualities to those closest to you, what qualities would you most want to leave them?

2. What is the "greater and more perfect tabernacle" that the author is referring to (v. 11; 8:1–2; 9:1–10)?

3. According to the author, why is the blood of Christ better than the blood of goats and bulls to spiritually cleanse a person?

4. What has to happen before a will is put in place? Why is this important to the author's argument?

5. What did Moses have to sprinkle with blood under the old covenant? Why does that have significant implications for the new covenant?

6. Why is it that the priests under the old covenant had to offer sacrifices again and again, while Christ only had to sacrifice himself once?

7. How will the second coming of Christ differ in nature and purpose from his first?

8. How well prepared are you right now to face death and judgment (v. 27)? If you knew you had only one week to live, what would you do differently?

GOING DEEPER: *If your group has time and/or wants a challenge, go on to this question.*

9. Why does blood have to be shed in order for there to be forgiveness (v. 22; Lev. 4–7; Rom. 6:23; 1 Peter 1:18–19)?

CARING TIME   15 Min.
APPLY THE LESSON AND PRAY FOR ONE ANOTHER

LEADER

Have you identified someone in the group that could be a leader for a new small group when your group divides? How could you encourage and mentor that person?

For us to thrive as Christians, we need more than study— we need support and encouragement. This is your time to give that to each other. Share your responses to the following questions before closing in prayer.

1. What do you look forward to the most about these meetings?

2. What is something you can do in the coming week to "serve the living God" (v. 14)?

3. What act or attitude would you like to "cleanse your conscience" of right now? How can this group help?

NEXT WEEK

Today we considered why it is essential to our salvation that Christ was willing to sacrifice his life and blood for the forgiveness of our sins. In the coming week, take some extra time at the end of each day to reflect on how much Jesus loves you and to thank him for the sacrifice he made. Next week we will look at how that sacrifice gives us confidence before God, and helps us to persevere in difficult times.

NOTES ON HEBREWS 9:11–28

Summary: In this section of Hebrews, the author switches his focus from Christ as high priest to Christ as the sacrifice that he himself offers. This concept would have been seen as nothing short of revolutionary by most of the Jews of the time. There was nothing more central to Hebrew worship than the offering of sacrifices for the sins of the people. And now they are being told that offering is no longer needed because Christ has done it once and for all. The temple, the building that was their pride and a central symbol of their faith and culture, was now without a function! We can talk glibly of how the Jewish religious establishment didn't recognize the Messiah when he came, but we need to recognize what a shocking perspective they were being asked to accept. Accepting Jesus as Messiah would mean changes that cut to the heart of their culture.

Still, there was continuity between the new covenant and the ancient traditions—both demanded a blood sacrifice as a prerequisite to forgiveness: "... without the shedding of blood there is no forgiveness" (v. 22). In today's culture this idea is often difficult to accept. Many people question, "Why is that? Isn't God a loving, forgiving God? Why does he need to see blood shed in order to forgive? A truly forgiving human doesn't make this requirement!" But we cannot put the God of the universe on the same plane as ordinary mortals. God is a holy God and he demands holy behavior. Sometimes as humans we want easy forgiveness. No matter what we have done wrong—cheated on our spouse, abused our children, destroyed our family through an addiction—we want to be able to just say "sorry" and forget about it. But even as humans most of us realize that such an easy out cheapens the value of those we have deeply hurt. If we realize the perils of forgiveness that comes too cheaply when we have hurt people, how much more should we realize this when the one we have injured is the God of creation? That is what this section of Hebrews is really about.

9:11 *the greater ... tabernacle.* In contrast to the temple worship, Jesus entered a "tabernacle" that is not part of the sin-infected creation.

9:12 *once for all.* The finality of Christ's ministry stands in marked contrast to the ongoing cycle of sacrifices represented by the Day of Atonement in the old covenant: Christ was sacrificed once for all (v. 26); he brought the blood of his sacrifice into God's presence once for all; his sacrifice secures the forgiveness of the sins of his people once for all (10:10). ***eternal redemption.*** The Day of Atonement brought freedom from ceremonial uncleanness, but, as time wore on, the people were again defiled and needed another act of redemption the following year. The liberation from sin that Christ has secured is, by contrast, spiritual and permanent.

9:13 *The blood of goats and bulls.* A reference to the sacrifices on the Day of Atonement (Lev. 16). ***ashes of a heifer.*** Israelites who were ceremonially defiled through contact with a dead body were cleansed by being sprinkled with water mixed with the ashes of a burned heifer. Without this cleansing, they could not worship at the tabernacle (Num. 19). ***outwardly clean.*** Literally, "cleanness of the flesh," set in opposition to the cleanness of the spirit (v. 14; Matt. 23:26).

9:14 *How much more.* If the sacrifice of an animal could bring about some change in a person's standing with God, obviously the sacrifice of the royal Son of God would be more effective! *the blood of Christ.* Blood represents sacrifice and death. *the eternal Spirit.* Literally, "an eternal spirit." This does not refer to the Holy Spirit, but to Christ's eternal nature (7:16). Because Christ himself is eternal in nature, the redemption he secured is likewise everlasting (v. 12). The phrase also contrasts the spiritual nature of Christ's sacrifice to the fleshly nature of the old (v. 13). While they only ceremonially cleansed the body, the new sacrifice actually cleanses the conscience. *unblemished.* Sacrificial animals had to be of the best quality. What was true of them physically was true of Christ morally in that he was without sin (4:15). *acts that lead to death.* Literally, "dead works." The old sacrifices cleansed a person defiled by contact with a dead body; the new sacrifice cleanses a person from a life of sin, which leads to death.

9:15 *died as a ransom.* Who demanded the ransom? While it is not said specifically here, it could be seen as Satan (2:14–15).

9:19 *blood of calves.* The Greek text adds "and goats." Several accounts in which blood is associated with covenant-making or cleansing are combined (Gen. 15:9; Ex. 24:1–8; Lev. 14:6–7).

9:20 *This is the blood.* This paraphrase of Exodus 24:8 would remind the readers of Jesus' words as he instituted the new covenant (Matt. 26:28).

9:22 *without the shedding of blood.* This is the main point of the argument. Just as there is no inheritance from a will without a death, so the covenant promises cannot be fulfilled without a sacrifice. God accepts the death of the sacrifice in place of the deserved death of the sinner (Lev. 17:11).

9:24 *he entered heaven itself.* Paul saw the Ascension as the exaltation of Jesus as King (Phil. 2:9–10). This author, in keeping with the priestly theme, sees it as Jesus' entry into the heavenly Most Holy Place.

9:28 *appear a second time.* Unlike the old high priests, Christ will not have to come again to bear sin yet another year. Instead, he will come to usher in the fullness of salvation.

A CALL TO PERSEVERE

SCRIPTURE HEBREWS 10:19–39

LAST WEEK

In last week's session we considered how Christ's blood sacrifice replaced all other sacrifices under the old covenant, and once and for all brought us the forgiveness of our sins. This unconditional forgiveness provided a way to a new covenant and relationship with God. This week we will see how Christ's blood can give us confidence before God, and how that confidence can in turn help us to persevere in hard times.

ICE-BREAKER   15 Min.
CONNECT WITH YOUR GROUP

LEADER

Choose one or two of the Ice-Breaker questions. If you have a new group member you may want to do all three. Remember to stick closely to the three-part agenda and the time allowed for each segment.

"Into every life a little rain must fall." This is an old, but truthful cliché. We have all gone through hard times—some because of our own poor choices. Take turns sharing your experiences with "rain" in your life, whether through circumstances beyond your control or your own moral choices.

1. When you were in grade school and had to approach your parents to talk to them about something you had done wrong, how confidently did you approach them?
    ❑ Only with fear and trembling.
    ❑ Only after all other options were used up.
    ❑ With full confidence that they would hear and care.
    ❑ Other _____.

2. What act did you commit as a child in grade school that you felt guilty about for a long time—and perhaps even still feel a little guilty about?

3. When you were an adolescent, what was the biggest test of your ability to persevere?

❏ Getting through school.

❏ Football workouts.

❏ Living with your parents.

❏ Tolerating the behavior of a sibling.

❏ Other _____.

BIBLE STUDY   30 Min.
READ SCRIPTURE AND DISCUSS

LEADER

Ask a member of the group, selected ahead of time, to read the Scripture passage. Then discuss the Questions for Interaction, dividing into subgroups of four or five.

The author returns now to the "bottom line" of what he has been trying to say: the readers should not "fold" in the midst of hard times, but should hold true to faith in their Savior. If they fail to do so, they will certainly be judged. Read Hebrews 10:19–39 and note the rewards that await those who persevere.

A Call to Persevere

¹⁹Therefore, brothers, since we have confidence to enter the Most Holy Place by the blood of Jesus, ²⁰by a new and living way opened for us through the curtain, that is, his body, ²¹and since we have a great priest over the house of God, ²²let us draw near to God with a sincere heart in full assurance of faith, having our hearts sprinkled to cleanse us from a guilty conscience and having our bodies washed with pure water. ²³Let us hold unswervingly to the hope we profess, for he who promised is faithful. ²⁴And let us consider how we may spur one another on toward love and good deeds. ²⁵Let us not give up meeting together, as some are in the habit of doing, but let us encourage one another—and all the more as you see the Day approaching.

²⁶If we deliberately keep on sinning after we have received the knowledge of the truth, no sacrifice for sins is left, ²⁷but only a fearful expectation of judgment and of raging fire that will consume the enemies of God. ²⁸Anyone who rejected the law of Moses died without mercy on the testimony of two or three witnesses. ²⁹How much more severely do you think a man deserves to be punished who has trampled the Son of God under foot, who has treated as an unholy thing the blood of the covenant that sanctified him, and who has insulted the Spirit of grace? ³⁰For we know him who said, "It is mine to avenge; I will repay," and again, "The Lord will judge his people." ³¹It is a dreadful thing to fall into the hands of the living God.

³²Remember those earlier days after you had received the light, when you stood your ground in a great contest in the face of suffering. *[33]Sometimes you were publicly exposed to insult and persecution; at other times you stood side by side with those who were so treated.[34]You sympathized with those in prison and joyfully accepted the confiscation of your property, because you knew that you yourselves had better and lasting possessions.*

[35]So do not throw away your confidence; it will be richly rewarded. [36]You need to persevere so that when you have done the will of God, you will receive what he has promised. [37]For in just a very little while,

"He who is coming will come and will not delay.
[38]But my righteous one will live by faith.
And if he shrinks back,
I will not be pleased with him."
[39]But we are not of those who shrink back and are destroyed, but of those who believe and are saved.

Hebrews 10:19–39

QUESTIONS FOR INTERACTION

LEADER

Refer to the Summary and Study Notes at the end of this session as needed. If 30 minutes is not enough time to answer all of the questions in this section, conclude the Bible Study by answering question #7.

1. What four actions should we be doing, given the truth of what the author has been saying about Christ's work as high priest? Which of these four actions do you do best? Which do you need to work on?

2. What does the author refer to as "the curtain"? What is the curtain to? What does it mean that he refers to it in this way?

3. What should we expect if we turn away from the truth of what God has done in Jesus Christ?

4. What are some important reasons why people shouldn't "give up meeting together" (v. 25)? What makes some people turn away from a church fellowship? How could they be encouraged?

5. What had the readers gone through because of their faith? What caring ministries had they performed? Why is the author having them recall this time?

6. What do you remember when you think back on the "earlier days after you had received the light" of the Gospel? How did you feel about your new faith? What did you do to express that faith?

7. What challenges are you meeting in your life that make it more difficult to persevere in your faith? What is helping you get past those challenges?

GOING DEEPER: *If your group has time and/or wants a challenge, go on to this question.*

8. How do you reconcile the Christian message that "God is love" (1 John 4:8), with the message that "It is a dreadful thing to fall into the hands of the living God" (v. 31; see also Hos. 11:1–11, where the tension between God's love and judgment is highlighted)?

CARING TIME   15 Min.

APPLY THE LESSON AND PRAY FOR ONE ANOTHER

LEADER

Conclude the group prayer today by reading 1 Timothy 6:11–12a: *But you, man [and woman] of God, flee from all this, and pursue righteousness, godliness, faith, love, endurance and gentleness. Fight the good fight of the faith. Take hold of the eternal life to which you were called ....*

Begin this Caring Time by sharing your responses to the following questions. Then take some time to share prayer requests and pray for one another.

1. On a scale of 1 (very little) to 10 (very much), how much confidence do you have in your faith right now and the ability to persevere when times get hard?

2. How can you spur another Christian on toward love and good deeds in the coming week?

3. In what way can this group "stand side by side" with you this week (v. 33)?

NEXT WEEK

This week we were reminded once again of the rewards that await those who persevere in their faith, and the judgment that awaits those who "shrink back" from a faith that once meant a great deal to them (v. 39). In the coming week, ask God to put someone on your heart that may be struggling with his or her faith. Then follow up with an encouraging phone call or letter to that person. Next week we will consider some examples of people whose faith in hard times was exemplary. It is the best-known chapter of Hebrews, and provides a challenging picture of what true faith is.

70

NOTES ON HEBREWS 10:19–39

Summary: Previous to this section the author has been focusing on who Christ is, in particular his role as God's great high priest and sacrifice. Now in this section he begins to focus on what we should do in response to Christ and his sacrifice. We should "draw near to God" (v. 22), "hold unswervingly to the hope we profess" (v. 23), "spur one another on toward love and good deeds" (v. 24), and "not give up meeting together" (v. 25). All of this is important because it helps keep us from falling away from the faith; a danger that the author feels threatens this community of believers. So to motivate them to stay true he does three things. He reminds them of what Christ has done (all the previous chapters, summarized in vv. 19–21); he points out the penalties awaiting those who aren't true (vv. 26–31); and he seeks to encourage them by reminding them of the faithful things they had done in the past (vv. 32–34). An essential part of this latter positive approach is claiming a positive mutual identity: "But we are not of those who shrink back and are destroyed, but of those who believe and are saved" (v. 39).

10:19 *Therefore ...* The author starts in on the practical implications of what he has been saying. ***enter the Most Holy Place.*** In the old covenant only the high priest could draw near to God. In contrast, all Christians can do so with assurance. ***by the blood of Jesus.*** As the high priest entered the Most Holy Place bearing a sacrifice, so Christians draw near to God through the sacrifice of Jesus.

10:20 that is, his body. Jesus' body, like the curtain of the temple, needed to be torn to provide access to God's presence forever. However, given that the curtain blocked the entrance to God's presence (9:8), the phrase may be better understood when linked to the "new and living way." In this reading, the bodily sacrifice of Jesus is the way through the curtain into God's presence.

10:22–25 *hearts sprinkled.* Priestly garments were consecrated for use by being sprinkled with the blood of a sacrifice (Ex. 29:19–21). This external consecration points to the internal consecration of the

believer through Christ. The author goes on to give a fourfold admonition, each beginning with the words, "Let us." ***let us draw near to God.*** This is the admonition to faith. This should include freedom from a guilty conscience. ***Let us hold unswervingly to the hope we profess.*** This is the admonition to hope. It is an essential thing to say to people who the author expects will be facing persecution, when it will be difficult to hope. ***And let us consider how we may spur one another on toward love and good deeds.*** This is the admonition to love. These first three replicate the three virtues Paul referred to in 1 Corinthians 13. But there is another. ***Let us not give up meeting together.*** After faith, hope and love, we also need discipline—the discipline of meeting together with other Christians who can love and support us. The concern here is not just a matter of missing an occasional church meeting, but of turning away from the community as a whole.

10:26 *deliberately keep on sinning.* A conscious choice to deliberately and persistently pursue a path that violates God's will. ***no***

sacrifice for sins is left. The Levitical sacrifices covered ceremonial uncleanness, moral lapses for which one repented (Lev. 6:1–7), and sins of ignorance and passion (Lev. 5:17–19; 19:20–22). Sins that were a defiant rejection of the Law were not covered by the sacrifices (Num. 15:30). The author transfers this principle to the new covenant as well. The God-appointed sacrifice must be met with an attitude of repentance and dedication. To reject Christ's sacrifice is to reject the *only* sacrifice for sins.

10:28 *rejected the law of Moses.* The concern here is not simply with breaking one of the commands of the Law, but of setting it aside as having no validity—such as a Jew who violated the essence of Israel's covenant with God by embracing idolatry (Deut. 17:2–7).

10:29 *trampled the Son of God/treated as an unholy thing the blood of the covenant/insulted the Spirit of grace.* These three phrases amplify the nature of the sin warned against. It is a deliberate rejection of Jesus as the Messiah, a decision to abandon the covenant that comes through his sacrifice, and a resistance to the Spirit who applies God's grace to those who trust.

10:32 *in a great contest.* Jewish Christians were most likely the recipients of this letter. They had probably suffered persecution from their fellow Jews. This ranged from harassment (Acts 18:17), to murder (Acts 7:59). Some experienced family rejection, economic boycotts and physical abuse leading to forced relocation and the resultant loss of property (Acts 8:1). The image of an athletic contest is used to describe the conflict.

10:33–34 These people risked standing with those being persecuted in spite of the danger to themselves. It is this type of dedication that they are being called to display once more (Matt. 5:11–12).

10:35 *confidence.* This is the same word translated as "courage" in Hebrews 3:6. ***rewarded.*** Jesus promises a great reward for those who endure suffering for his sake (Matt 5:12).

10:37–38 *in just a very little while.* A slightly rearranged version of Habakkuk 2:3–4 (from the Greek Septuagint) is quoted to support the author's call for perseverance in faith. The Lord is coming, therefore do not shrink back and meet with God's displeasure.

SESSION 11
MODELS OF FAITH

SCRIPTURE HEBREWS 11:1,6–16,32–40

LAST WEEK

In our last session together we considered the importance of persevering in our faith despite the trials and persecution we might face. We were also reminded how we need the support of other Christians in order to help us to persevere. This week the author has us look at some biblical examples of people whose faith in hard times was exemplary. The faith of these people helps us to define faith, not in terms of words, but in terms of lives lived. Let's look at their example and see what they have to teach us.

ICE-BREAKER   15 Min.
CONNECT WITH YOUR GROUP

. . . .

LEADER

Choose one, two or all three Ice-Breaker questions, depending on your group's needs.

The places we go and the people we meet on our journey through life all shape who we are today. Those who have gone before us in the faith can also guide us by their example. Before we look at these biblical lives of faith, let's take turns sharing about some people and places from our own past.

1. Who were your biggest heroes when you were in grade school? What feats or powers did you especially admire them for?

2. When you were first starting out as a young adult, what were some of the places like where you lived? What challenges did living at these places present to you?

3. What country do you most long to visit? What would you look forward to seeing and doing there?

BIBLE STUDY

READ SCRIPTURE AND DISCUSS

30 Min.

LEADER

Select two members of the group ahead of time to read aloud the Scripture passage. Have one person read verses 1,6–16, and the other read verses 32–40. Then discuss the Questions for Interaction, dividing into subgroups of four or five.

In today's reading the author calls us to greater faith by highlighting some of the biblical characters who demonstrated incredible faith in God. These people can serve as inspirational examples to us. Read Hebrews 11:1,6–16,32–40 and note how each person lived out their faith and the amazing miracles that resulted from that faith.

By Faith

Reader 1: **11** *Now faith is being sure of what we hope for and certain of what we do not see.... ⁶And without faith it is impossible to please God, because anyone who comes to him must believe that he exists and that he rewards those who earnestly seek him. ⁷By faith Noah, when warned about things not yet seen, in holy fear built an ark to save his family. By his faith he condemned the world and became heir of the righteousness that comes by faith.*

⁸By faith Abraham, when called to go to a place he would later receive as an inheritance, obeyed and went, even though he did not know where he was going. ⁹By faith he made his home in the promised land like a stranger in a foreign country; he lived in tents, as did Isaac and Jacob, who were heirs with him of the same promise. ¹⁰For he was looking forward to the city with foundations, whose architect and builder is God.

¹¹By faith Abraham, even though he was past age— and Sarah herself was barren—was enabled to become a father because he considered him faithful who had made the promise. ¹²And so from this one man, and he as good as dead, came descendants as numerous as the stars in the sky and as countless as the sand on the seashore.

¹³All these people were still living by faith when they died. They did not receive the things promised; they only saw them and welcomed them from a distance. And they admitted that they were aliens and strangers on earth. ¹⁴People who say such things show that they are looking for a country of their own. ¹⁵If they had been thinking of the country they had left, they would have had opportunity to return. ¹⁶Instead, they were longing for a better country—a heavenly one. Therefore God is not ashamed to be called their God, for he has prepared a city for them....

Reader 2: [32] *And what more shall I say? I do not have time to tell about Gideon, Barak, Samson, Jephthah, David, Samuel and the prophets,* [33] *who through faith conquered kingdoms, administered justice, and gained what was promised; who shut the mouths of lions,* [34] *quenched the fury of the flames, and escaped the edge of the sword; whose weakness was turned to strength; and who became powerful in battle and routed foreign armies.* [35] *Women received back their dead, raised to life again. Others were tortured and refused to be released, so that they might gain a better resurrection.* [36] *Some faced jeers and flogging, while still others were chained and put in prison.* [37] *They were stoned; they were sawed in two; they were put to death by the sword. They went about in sheepskins and goatskins, destitute, persecuted and mistreated*—[38] *the world was not worthy of them. They wandered in deserts and mountains, and in caves and holes in the ground.*

[39] *These were all commended for their faith, yet none of them received what had been promised.* [40] *God had planned something better for us so that only together with us would they be made perfect.*

Hebrews 11:1,6–16, 32–40

LEADER

Refer to the Summary and Study Notes at the end of this session as needed. If 30 minutes is not enough time to answer all of the questions in this section, conclude the Bible Study by answering question #7.

QUESTIONS FOR INTERACTION

1. Of the people mentioned by the author, whose faith has the most significance to you? Who might you add to this list from your own personal spiritual history?

2. How does the author define faith? How do you see the factors he mentions in the actions of the people to whom he refers?

3. What two truths does a person who is seeking God need to believe (v. 6)? Have there been times in your life when you doubted either one of these truths? What, if anything, has helped you deal with that doubt?

4. How did these people of faith look upon their status on earth (v. 13)? What does this say about where they viewed their true home to be?

5. Which of the following acts of faith told of in this chapter would you find hardest to do?
❏ Moving to a strange land at God's request.
❏ Believing an impossible promise of a child in old age.
❏ Facing a painful death.
❏ Believing a dead loved one will live again.
❏ Facing jeers and social persecution.

6. What point is the author trying to make by repeating that even though these people had great faith, they did not receive what God promised in their lifetime (vv. 13,39)? What exactly was this promise?

7. What is the biggest challenge that your faith is facing right now?

GOING DEEPER: *If your group has time and/or wants a challenge, go on to this question.*

8. If Christians are truly "aliens and strangers on earth" (v. 13), what does that say about how attached we are to become to the things of this earth? Can (and should) we become attached to things that are part of a temporary sojourn?

CARING TIME   15 Min.
APPLY THE LESSON AND PRAY FOR ONE ANOTHER

LEADER

Conclude the prayer time today by asking God for guidance in determining the future mission and outreach of this group.

Recalling the great stories of men and women of faith can give us hope to carry on today. We can also get inspiration from each other in this important time of sharing and prayer.

1. How has God been at work in your life this past week?

2. Share about a time when your faith saw you through a difficult situation. What was the outcome?

3. How can this group pray for you in the midst of the challenge you shared about in question #7 under the Questions for Interaction?

NEXT WEEK

Today we were reminded of the importance of faith and the miracles that can happen if we truly believe in what God can do. Many who have gone before us have lived out this faith, and we had the opportunity today to be inspired by the examples of some of these great people of faith. In the coming week, express your gratitude to someone who has mentored you and helped your faith to grow. Next week the author will have us considering what the examples of these people can mean to us as we "run our race" toward the goal of sharing in Christ's kingdom.

NOTES ON HEBREWS 11:1,6–16,32–40

Summary: In the previous chapter, the author began focusing on what we should do in response to who Christ is and what he has done, and he continues that focus in this most famous of chapters in the book of Hebrews. We are above all called to a response of faith. But some might ask, "What do you mean by faith?" That would be a natural question. When Jesus called people to love their neighbors the question came up, "Who is my neighbor?" (Luke 10:29). Jesus responded with a concrete example. In the same way, the author here responds with some concrete examples of what faith is. He goes through the Bible in historical order, telling how various people gave living examples of faith. The list includes some examples that may be surprising. The sole example of a woman that is specifically named is the prostitute Rahab (v. 31)! However, the absence of someone like Deborah may equally surprise us since the list includes Barak (v. 32). Barak refused to go into battle unless Deborah was with him! (Judg. 4:8–9). Nevertheless, the impact of these examples of faith is uplifting. The author was saying, "These were people just like you, and look how their faith saw them through some pretty tough experiences!" But there is another point he is making as well. These people showed faith even though God was not ready to reward them with the fullness of the hope that later became available through Jesus Christ. People who knew of this hope, specifically the readers of this letter, should be all the more willing to follow in the faithful footsteps of those who had gone before them.

11:1 The call to live by faith (10:37–39) leads into a collection of stories of faithful people in the past designed to encourage the readers to be faithful in the present (12:1). **certain of what we do not see.** The essence of the modern secular perspective is, "What is real is what can be perceived by one of our five senses." But this passage declares quite the opposite, and more and more people have started to understand why. First of all, not all that our senses tell us reflects reality. If you put a pencil in a glass of water, it will appear to be broken, even though it is not. If you amputate a person's arm, they will often sense that it is still there, even though it is not. Also, not all that is real can be sensed with one of our five senses. Modern science is built on what cannot be seen directly—black holes and electrons are good examples from the opposite ends of the size spectrum. God is the ultimate reality in this category. We do not see God directly, but (like with black holes and electrons) only his effect on the world. What the author says here also fits well into his Platonic perspective—the visible, touchable world is a shadow of a higher reality. Paul also affirms this perspective on "things not seen" in Romans 8:24–25.

11:6 This is the core verse of the chapter. The second part that says God "rewards those who earnestly seek him" is vital. Here we learn that the person who earnestly seeks God can find him. This is a message of hope that assures the seeker God is not "playing hide and seek," and that he will reward his or her efforts.

11:7 Noah. Noah's faith is not mentioned in the Old Testament, but is seen in his obedience to God (Gen. 6:8–9:17). **not yet seen.** Acting upon that which God promises (or warns), even when unseen, is the essence of faith (v. 1). **in holy fear.** Faith lives in recognition of the awesome power of God.

condemned the world. Noah condemned the world in that he acted in obedience to God while others did not.

11:9–10 In contrast to his settled life in Ur, Abraham's nomadic life in Canaan showed that his eyes were fixed upon a vision of something greater than could be found in this world.

11:12 and he as good as dead. Abraham was 99 years old when God gave him the child through whom he would make good on his promise to make a great nation of him.

11:13 All these people. Abraham, Sarah, Isaac, Jacob. **living by faith when they died.** None of the patriarchs saw the fulfillment of God's promise regarding the land or the vast nation Abraham would father. **aliens and strangers.** Both terms describe how believers are to view their lives in the world (John 17:14).

11:16 called their God. God openly identifies with these people, pledging himself to them (Ex. 3:6,15).

11:33–34 There are three sets of three items from this catalog of faith deeds: The first triplet concerns events that affected Israel as a whole; the second triplet considers stories of dramatic personal deliverance; the third triplet looks at examples of power released through faith.

11:33 conquered kingdoms. David's conquests are probably in mind (2 Sam. 1–10). **administered justice.** Both Samuel and David were renowned for their justice as leaders in Israel (1 Sam. 12:3–5; 2 Sam. 8:15). **gained what was promised.** Under David, Israel was a mighty nation that possessed the land promised to Abraham.

11:34 quenched the fury of the flames. Shadrach, Meshach and Abednego must be in view (Dan. 3). **escaped ... the sword.** This may refer to David's several close calls at being killed by Saul (1 Sam. 18:10–11; 19:11–12; 23:26–27). **weakness was turned to strength.** Samson may be in mind (Judg. 16:28). **powerful in battle.** David's exploits were legendary (1 Sam. 17; 18:7). **routed foreign armies.** This, as well as many of the examples in verses 35–38, probably refers to the Jewish heroes during the Maccabean revolt against the Seleucids in second century B.C.

11:35 Women received back their dead. See 1 Kings 17:17–24 and 2 Kings 4:11–37.

11:36 jeers/prison. While this applies to the Maccabean heroes, Jeremiah the prophet also comes to mind (Jer. 20:2; 38:6).

11:37 stoned/sawed in two. Tradition held that Jeremiah was stoned in Egypt and that Isaiah was sawn in two by the evil king Manasseh. **put to death by the sword.** Uriah, a prophet contemporary with Jeremiah, met this end (Jer. 26:20–23).

11:38 the world was not worthy of them. The qualities of integrity and courage these people displayed put the rest of scheming, compromising humanity to shame. **wandered in ... caves.** Jews during the Maccabean revolt hid out in caves around Palestine.

11:39 commended. Literally, "obtained a witness," in that their stories were recorded for future generations. **none ... received what had been promised.** They never personally experienced the "heavenly rest.'

SESSION 12
THE DISCIPLINE OF THE RACE

SCRIPTURE HEBREWS 12:1–13

LAST WEEK

Faith was the topic for our session last week, and we were reminded of what faith truly means and how we are to live out that faith in our everyday lives. The author of Hebrews helped us to understand this by giving some inspirational examples of great people of faith in the Bible. This week we will look at what these examples mean for us as we seek to "run the race" toward the goal of being part of Christ's kingdom. We will also consider the discipline God sends our way to keep us on course.

ICE-BREAKER   15 Min.
CONNECT WITH YOUR GROUP

LEADER

Choose one, two or all three of the Ice-Breaker questions, depending on your group's needs.

Even though we may not appreciate it at the time, discipline is an important part of growing and learning. We need discipline in many areas of our lives, including physical, emotional and spiritual areas. Take turns sharing your unique life experiences with discipline.

1. When you were a child, what disciplinary technique did your parent(s) use on you most frequently, and how did you react to their disciplinary methods?
   ❐ Spanking.
   ❐ Time out.
   ❐ Taking away privileges.
   ❐ Grounding you.

2. When you were a child, what activities did you and your friends or siblings turn into a race?
   ❐ Getting chores done.
   ❐ Finishing a puzzle.
   ❐ Getting to your favorite gathering spot.
   ❐ Other _____.

3. What discipline do you find to be most painful at this time of your life?
❏ Exercising.
❏ Watching what you eat.
❏ Being spiritually accountable.
❏ Other _____.

BIBLE STUDY 30 Min.
READ SCRIPTURE AND DISCUSS

LEADER

Select a member of the group ahead of time to read aloud the Scripture passage. Then discuss the Questions for Interaction, dividing into subgroups of four or five.

The author pictures the people discussed in the previous chapter as spectators of a race that Christians of his time were running. Those people of faith were cheering them on, as they ran toward the goal of being like Christ. In that race there would need to be discipline if they were to win. Since we are now the ones "running the race" we need to learn from their experience and achieve the same discipline. Read Hebrews 12:1–13 and note how we are to react when the Lord disciplines us.

God Disciplines His Sons

12 *Therefore, since we are surrounded by such a great cloud of witnesses, let us throw off everything that hinders and the sin that so easily entangles, and let us run with perseverance the race marked out for us. ²Let us fix our eyes upon Jesus, the author and perfecter of our faith, who for the joy set before him endured the cross, scorning its shame, and sat down at the right hand of the throne of God. ³Consider him who endured such opposition from sinful men, so that you will not grow weary and lose heart.*

⁴In your struggle against sin, you have not yet resisted to the point of shedding your blood. ⁵And you have forgotten that word of encouragement that addresses you as sons:

"My son, do not make light of the Lord's discipline,
and do not lose heart when he rebukes you,
⁶because the Lord disciplines those he loves,
and he punishes everyone he accepts as a son."

⁷Endure hardship as discipline; God is treating you as sons. For what son is not disciplined by his father? ⁸If you are not disciplined (and everyone undergoes discipline), then you are illegitimate children and not true sons. ⁹Moreover, we have all had human fathers who disciplined us and we respected them for it.

How much more should we submit to the Father of our spirits and live! ¹⁰Our fathers disciplined us for a little while as they thought best; but God disciplines us for our good, that we may share in his holiness. ¹¹No discipline seems pleasant at the time, but painful. Later on, however, it produces a harvest of righteousness and peace for those who have been trained by it.

¹²Therefore, strengthen your feeble arms and weak knees. ¹³ "Make level paths for your feet," so that the lame may not be disabled, but rather healed.

Hebrews 12:1–13

QUESTIONS FOR INTERACTION

LEADER

Refer to the Summary and Study Notes at the end of this session as needed. If 30 minutes is not enough time to answer all of the questions in this section, conclude the Bible Study by answering question #7.

1. What part of this passage do you relate to most strongly?
   ❏ Having people watch you run a race (vv. 1–2).
   ❏ Dealing with opposition from sinful people (v. 3).
   ❏ Having respect for a parent who disciplined you (v. 9).
   ❏ The unpleasantness of being disciplined (v. 11).

2. What garments might hinder a runner who is trying to run a race? How does the author see sin as being like such garments?

3. Where should we be fixing our eyes while we are running our "race"? Why is this important?

4. Why should the readers consider how Jesus endured opposition from sinful men? What relevance might such a consideration have to their own situation?

5. How should the readers view the hardships they are going through? What does it say about their relationship to God the Father?

6. When has something happened to you that, while painful, later turned out to provide a strengthening discipline to your life?

7. In what current situation do you need to "strengthen your feeble arms and weak knees" in order to face it (v. 12)? Where are you looking to find that strength?

GOING DEEPER: *If your group has time and/or wants a challenge, go on to this question.*

8. What makes the difference between those who go through hardship and come out of it with "a harvest of righteousness and peace," and those who only harvest anger and bitterness?

CARING TIME   15 Min.
APPLY THE LESSON AND PRAY FOR ONE ANOTHER

LEADER

Following the Caring Time, discuss with your group how they would like to celebrate the last session next week. Also, discuss the possibility of splitting into two groups and continuing with another study.

"Let us fix our eyes on Jesus" (v. 2) and support one another with a time of sharing and prayer, "so that you will not grow weary and lose heart" (v. 3).

1. What is something for which you are particularly thankful?

2. What are two obstacles that hinder and entangle you in your race? Why?

3. How can this group pray for you in the midst of the challenge that you shared about in question #7 under Questions for Interaction?

NEXT WEEK

Today we looked at a difficult, but necessary topic—how God disciplines his children. We were reminded that God disciplines us because he loves us and wants to help us produce "a harvest of righteousness and peace" (v. 11). In the coming week, reflect each evening on what God was teaching you through the difficult times you faced during the day's activities. Next week will be our final session in this study. We will examine some of the author's closing exhortations to help us live in the light of God's kingdom. Those exhortations will include a reassurance to readers that his kingdom is one that cannot be shaken.

NOTES ON HEBREWS 12:1–13

Summary: After surveying great people of faith in the last chapter, the author now goes on to use an extended metaphor concerning how we should respond to these examples of faith. The metaphor is one of a race. The people of faith who have gone before us are those in the crowd, cheering the runners on (v. 1). The runners are Christians of the author's day. They are called to keep their eyes fixed on the goal of the race, which is Jesus Christ (v. 2). They are to accept discipline as the training they need to win the race (vv. 7–11). They should do all they can to strengthen themselves for this very important race (v. 12).

These admonitions are all important because the people to whom this author is writing are facing the prospects of persecution, a persecution which could well try them in ways they have not been tried to this point (v. 4). The whole letter has been an effort to keep them from turning away from their faith during such a time. They have been urged to remember who Christ is and what he has done for them (ch. 1–10). They have been warned of the penalties of falling away (3:7–19; 10:19–31). And they have been pointed toward the examples of other people of faith who have gone before them (ch. 11). Now in this pivotal chapter, they are told to "run a good race" in the light of all they have been told. In many respects, this chapter is a lesson in the importance of Scripture to Christians of any age and time. We must learn the stories of those who have run before us, and use them to inspire us in running our own race.

12:1 *such a great cloud of witnesses.* The word "cloud" was a fairly common metaphor of the time for a large crowd of people. The crowd consists of the great people of faith referred to in chapter 11. The word for "witnesses" is the same word used for "martyrs." It is probably a deliberate play on words in which both meanings are intended. The vision is one of people in the stands at a race. It is as if the people of faith who have gone before us are in the stands cheering us on as we "run our race." Paul uses similar imagery in 1 Corinthians 9:24–27 and Philippians 3:12–14. ***throw off everything.*** This again is an allusion to a race where the runner strips down, and takes off all clothing that might encumber him, wearing only the essentials. In the Christian life it refers to getting rid of distracting or non-helpful habits or sins. ***the sin that so easily entangles.*** Just as a

flowing robe makes it impossible to run, so sin makes the Christian life difficult.

12:2 *fix our eyes on Jesus.* In races of the time, the prize for the race was placed at the end so that the runners raced with their eyes on the prize. This is certainly what Paul had in mind in Philippians 3:12–14, and probably also what the author of Hebrews had in mind here. The goal of our "race" is to be like Jesus. He is our prize and motivation. ***joy set before him.*** Jesus knew the joy his mission of reconciliation would bring, and so pursued it whatever the cost. The readers are to follow that model. ***scorning its shame.*** Crucifixion was considered so degrading that no Roman citizen could be crucified, regardless of the crime committed.

12:3 *Consider him.* Instead of seeing opposition as an excuse to abandon faith, they should look to Jesus as a model of how to live faithfully through it. ***weary and lose heart.*** These words were used in athletic circles to describe the collapse of a runner.

12:4 *shedding your blood.* The persecution they have experienced so far has not yet included the ultimate sacrifice made by Jesus. This is historically significant, showing that the author was not writing during one of the great persecutions, such as under Nero or Domitian.

12:6–11 *the Lord disciplines those he loves.* The author sees the hardship his readers are going through as part of God's discipline for them. He emphasizes that this is a good thing, because it is an indication of their status as God's children. A good parent always disciplines his or her children, and God is the best parent of all.

12:12–13 Returning to the image of a race, quotes from Isaiah 35:3 and Proverbs 4:26 encourage those who are getting weary to rouse themselves in their pursuit of Christ. The readers needed both internal and external changes in order to survive the tough times.

12:12 *strengthen your feeble arms and weak knees.* The readers needed to find strength in themselves. We can find this internal strength when we remember that the Holy Spirit is within us, and that God has gifted us.

12:13 *Make level paths for your feet.* The readers also needed to tend to their environment. Even a well-conditioned runner can injure himself or herself on ground that is full of rocks and holes and uneven places. We can find external strength by creating an environment that is conducive to morality. If a ghetto produces hate and violence, we can preach to the residents against hate and violence, but we also need to do something to change the environmental condition, to help them make a more level path for their feet.

A KINGDOM THAT CANNOT BE SHAKEN

SCRIPTURE HEBREWS 12:18–13:8

LAST WEEK

In our last session we looked at the role of God's discipline in the growth and development of our faith. This discipline may be painful at the time, but if we accept it and learn from it we will produce a "harvest of righteousness and peace" (12:11). We were also reminded of the people of faith who have gone before us, whose examples can help us to run the race of faith. In this final session we will examine some of the author's closing exhortations and be reassured that "we are receiving a kingdom that cannot be shaken" (12:28).

ICE-BREAKER   15 Min.
CONNECT WITH YOUR GROUP

LEADER

Begin this final session with a word of prayer and thanksgiving for this time together. Choose one or two Ice-Breaker questions to discuss.

Some events terrify us and make us shake. Others give us a sense of security or even joy. The author will talk about some of these things in the spiritual realm, but what about the things that have affected you throughout the course of your life? Take turns sharing your own personal history with the frightening and the reassuring.

1. What were you most terrified by when you were in grade school?
   ❏ Noises in the dark.
   ❏ A scowling teacher.
   ❏ A house that was said to be haunted.
   ❏ The neighborhood bully.
   ❏ Other _____.

2. What event do you remember "shaking your world" when you were a teenager?

❏ The death of a famous person (John Kennedy, Martin Luther King, Jr., Lennon, etc.).

❏ The news you were moving.

❏ A parent losing a job.

❏ Other _____.

3. As an adult, what do you like to rely on staying the same?

❏ Your morning routine.

❏ The television programs you watch.

❏ The style of worship at your church.

❏ Nothing.

BIBLE STUDY
Read Scripture and Discuss

30 Min.

LEADER

Select two members of the group ahead of time to read aloud the Scripture passage. Have one member read 12:18–29, and the other read 13:1–8. Then discuss the Questions for Interaction, dividing into subgroups of four or five.

Like many letters of the time, the author closes Hebrews with a variety of short admonitions. Many of them don't have much to do with the theme of the book. But there are also many thoughts that eloquently summarize what he has been saying all along. Read Hebrews 12:18–13:8 and note the many ways the author encourages his readers and us to choose "a kingdom that cannot be shaken."

A Kingdom That Cannot Be Shaken

Reader 1: *18You have not come to a mountain that can be touched and that is burning with fire; to darkness, gloom and storm; 19to a trumpet blast or to such a voice speaking words that those who heard it begged that no further word be spoken to them, 20because they could not bear what was commanded: "If even an animal touches the mountain, it must be stoned." 21The sight was so terrifying that Moses said, "I am trembling with fear."*

22But you have come to Mount Zion, to the heavenly Jerusalem, the city of the living God. You have come to thousands upon thousands of angels in joyful assembly, 23to the church of the firstborn, whose names are written in heaven. You have come to God, the judge of all men, to the spirits of righteous men made perfect, 24to Jesus the mediator of a new covenant, and to the sprinkled blood that speaks a better word than the blood of Abel.

25See to it that you do not refuse him who speaks. If they did not escape when they refused him who warned them on earth, how much less will we, if we turn away from him who warns us from heaven? 26At that time his voice shook the earth, but now he has promised, "Once more I will shake not only the earth but also the heavens." 27The words "once more" indicate the removing of what can be shaken—that is, created things—so that what cannot be shaken may remain.

28Therefore, since we are receiving a kingdom that cannot be shaken, let us be thankful, and so worship God acceptably with reverence and awe, 29for our "God is a consuming fire."

Reader 2:

13 *Keep on loving each other as brothers. 2Do not forget to entertain strangers, for by so doing some people have entertained angels without knowing it. 3Remember those in prison as if you were their fellow prisoners, and those who are mistreated as if you yourselves were suffering.*

4Marriage should be honored by all, and the marriage bed kept pure, for God will judge the adulterer and all the sexually immoral. 5Keep your lives free from the love of money and be content with what you have, because God has said,

"Never will I leave you;
never will I forsake you."

6So we say with confidence,

"The Lord is my helper; I will not be afraid.
What can man do to me?"

7Remember your leaders, who spoke the word of God to you. Consider the outcome of their way of life and imitate their faith. 8Jesus Christ is the same yesterday and today and forever.

Hebrews 12:18–13:8

LEADER

Refer to the Summary and Study Notes at the end of this session as needed. If 30 minutes is not enough time to answer all of the questions in this section, conclude the Bible Study by answering question #7.

QUESTIONS FOR INTERACTION

1. What biblical incident is the author referring to in 12:18–21? Why is he making a point of saying that is *not* the kind of experience they are coming to in Jesus Christ?

2. What are seven things that the readers *are* coming to (12:22–24)? How would you characterize the difference between what they are coming to and what they are not coming to?

3. What is the significance of the "shake down" that God will be doing on the created order (12:26–29)? What will survive this "shake down"?

4. Why does the author point out that "Jesus Christ is the same yesterday and today and forever" (13:8)? What implication does this have for the stresses they are going through?

5. Of the admonitions that the author gives in this section, which one do you do best? Which of these admonitions do you have the greatest difficulty with?
- ❏ Loving your brothers and sisters.
- ❏ Showing hospitality.
- ❏ Caring for those who are in prison or mistreated.
- ❏ Honoring marriage and family commitments.
- ❏ Being content with what you have.
- ❏ Honoring leaders.

6. Whose faith do you feel you would do well to imitate right now (13:7)?

7. What do you rely on in your world that you feel has been shaken recently? What message do you think God might be trying to give to you in the midst of this shaking?

GOING DEEPER: *If your group has time and/or wants a challenge, go on to this question.*

8. What are the implications for today's church that "Jesus Christ is the same yesterday and today and forever"? Does that mean that the way the church does things should never change?

CARING TIME   15 Min.
APPLY THE LESSON AND PRAY FOR ONE ANOTHER

LEADER

Conclude this final Caring Time by praying for each group member and asking for God's blessing in any plans to start a new group and/or continue to study together.

Gather around each other now in this final time of sharing and prayer and encourage one another to have faith as you go back out into the world, remembering that "The Lord is my helper; I will not be afraid" (13:6).

1. We are told to remember those who have spoken the word of God to us (13:7). How have people in this group spoken the word of God to you in the midst of these sessions?

2. What thrills you the most about one day living in the "heavenly Jerusalem, the city of the living God" (12:22)?

3. What will you remember most about this group? How would you like the group to continue to pray for you?

NOTES ON HEBREWS 12:18–13:8

Summary: We live in a day when everything seems to be constantly changing. Some of those changes are considered good by most people: the improvements in medical science, the increasing capabilities of computers to assist in learning and making work easier, the ability to be in touch with family members more easily through cell phone technology. However, there have been other changes, particularly changes in values and beliefs, which many of us don't see as being good at all. Our world, then, particularly needs to hear the message in this section that Jesus Christ is "the same yesterday and today and forever" (13:8). He is not like a car model that changes every year. He is one who consistently offers the same blessings of love and forgiveness—and who also consistently calls for the same kind of obedience.

Therefore, along with this comforting message that Jesus never changes, the author of Hebrews includes an emphasis that there are some values that need to remain the same: the sanctity of marriage (13:4), the shallowness of materialism (13:5), and the need to care for strangers and people in need (13:2), to name a few. Ignoring such values is not something we should expect God to take lightly. Rather, God is a God who will "shake the world" (12:26–29), and we need to maintain a system of values and beliefs that can stand up to that shaking. Obedience to Christ is what helps us to do that.

12:18–21 This retelling of the Israelites' experience at Mount Sinai is based on Exodus 19. The mood here is one of fear, because of the power and holiness of God. God's holiness was such that should even an animal touch the mountain, it would have to be stoned (Ex. 19:12–13).

12:22–24 The mood of this passage is joy (v. 22) rather than fear. The reason for the joy is a new relationship with God, where our sins are atoned for ("righteous men made perfect"), and accordingly we need not fear judgment. This is not because of our merit, but because of the work of Jesus Christ as mediator (v. 24). The author has spoken of this extensively in chapters 8–10. Our reward is the heavenly Jerusalem (v. 22), where we will receive heavenly rest the author had spoken of back in chapter 4.

12:24 *a better word than the blood of Abel.* The author had spoken of the importance of Christ's blood back in 10:11–28. Abel's blood was said to "cry out" to God from the ground (Gen. 4:10). Its word was a word of tragedy, sin and violation of God's good creation. Christ's blood, on the other hand, spoke of triumph, forgiveness and restoration of the goodness of creation.

12:25 *him who speaks.* That is, Jesus (v. 24). Since the royal Son and heavenly high priest addresses them, these people are even more obligated to heed God's Word than the Israelites at Mount Sinai.

12:26–27 Haggai 2:6 is a reminder that God will one day shake not only the earth (as at Mount Sinai), but also the heavens. Thus the old order, which is earthly, partial and temporary, will fully give way to the new, which is heavenly, complete and eternal. While the emphasis for those in Christ is joy rather than fear, should they turn from their faith in Christ they will once again have reason to fear if they "refuse him who speaks," because they will be part of that which will not remain.

12:28 *a kingdom.* This is the kingdom of God inaugurated by Jesus and consummated in the new heavens and new earth (Isa. 65:17–19; Mark 1:15; Rev. 21:1–7).

12:29 *a consuming fire.* The presence of God is frequently symbolized by fire in Scripture (Ex. 3:1–4; 13:20–22; Acts 2:3). Fire has the power to light and warm, or burn and destroy, and thus it represents God's power to love and guide, or judge in anger.

13:1 *loving each other as brothers.* Showing love to each other is one of the most consistent obligations put on the Christian (Matt. 22:34–40; 25:31–46; John 13:34–35; 1 John 4:7–12).

13:2 *entertained angels.* The idea that a stranger might be an angelic visitor stems back to Abraham and Lot (Gen. 18–19).

13:4 *Marriage.* The denial of legitimate sexual desire led to incidents of sexual immorality (1 Cor. 6:15–20). Here, marriage is validated and people are warned not to be involved in any form of immorality (12:16).

13:5 Economic oppression (10:34) may have created pressure to renounce the faith in order to restore financial security.

13:7 *Remember your leaders.* This refers to the people who introduced the readers to Jesus but were no longer with them.

13:8 The same trustworthy Jesus preached by the original leaders is the one the readers should continue to pursue "today and forever." Since Jesus and the Gospel are stable and eternal, the readers should not be distracted by any new teachings that differ from what they originally received (13:9).

Personal Notes

Personal Notes

Personal Notes

Personal Notes

Personal Notes